"The authors have superbly addressed the nature of change, associated obstacles, and the role of the school leader in implementing the change process. Most importantly, they provide specific management tools and interventions. As a prior school and district administrator, I highly recommend this book as a common sense approach. Even for those of us in organizations who are serious about remaining relevant and addressing the many generations represented, this book provides keen insight and tools needed."

Beverly Helms, EdD
International President, 2012–2014
The Delta Kappa Gamma Society International
Austin, TX

"What sets this work apart is that the authors compel us to examine the relationships among change initiatives, resource allocation and student achievement. They challenge us to ask, 'Would you invest in this idea?' A great read for school leaders everywhere!"

Julie Davis, EdD
Executive Director
Ohio Association of Elementary School Administrators

"*Leading School Change* provides a thorough review of the opportunities and challenges school leaders face when implementing change in their learning communities. Better yet, strategies and resources are offered to help school leaders navigate the change process successfully."

Jason Leahy
Executive Director
Illinois Principals Association

"Anyone who has been down the slippery slope of school change understands how complex and unpredictable it can be. This book helps unpack the variables, tactics and strategies to provide school leaders with a surer path to success. Their approach to understanding the process of change is dynamic and depends on building trust with all involved is right on target."

Fenwick W. English
R. Wendell Eaves Distinguished Professor of Educational Leadership
School of Education
University of North Carolina at Chapel Hill

"This is a 'must have' book for school leaders involved in school improvement planning."

Dr. Linda Marrs-Morford
Professor, Educational Leadership
Eastern Illinois University

"As a longtime student of the change process and an often-challenged leader in the process of educational change I find this book to be a directional beacon for change leadership. The inclusion of ELCC and ISLLC standard citations will be of great assistance to those needing to reference standards in their study or implementation. The inclusion of current organizational approaches in schools, such as PLCs, allows insights to where our educators are currently functioning in their institutions. I find this book to be a valuable resource to analyzing the change process for educational leaders."

D. William Dodds, EdD
Executive Director
Illinois ASCD

"*A must-read* for educational leaders and graduate students in all public and private educational arenas, *Leading School Change* is a ready-to-use, creative and compelling compendium of practical techniques and innovative approaches showing the learner how to generate commitment to change, sustain the collaborative change process and improve student performance."

Kenneth Jandes, EdD
Associate Dean
American College of Education
Indianapolis, IN

"Tomal, Schilling, and Trybus have tackled one of the most complex and challenging issues of education and do so in a way that is not only grounded in research and standards but practical and immediately relevant at the same time. This book should serve as a preamble for all school leaders and instructors of school leaders dealing with the challenges of change today."

Colin Cameron
Director of Programs
Confederation of Oregon School Administrators

"Drs. Tomal, Schilling and Trybus provide a streetwise yet theoretically accurate approach to leading school change. I highly recommend this book as a college-level textbook or as a reference guide for any school administrator."

Paul R. Erickson, PhD
Director
Educational Research, Assessment and Technology
Department of Educational Leadership and Policy Studies
Eastern Kentucky University

"Drs. Tomal, Schilling, and Trybus provide a thorough look at the complexities of leading school change. The strategies for involvement of all stakeholders in the process are comprehensive and practical. This book provides invaluable information for both practicing and aspiring school administrators. "

S. Murray, EdD
Associate Professor
University of Tennessee
Martin, TN

"In an academic environment faced with constant change at all levels of P–20 schools, *Leading School Change* provides readers an excellent source of leadership skills, intervention techniques, and implementation strategies needed for student success."

Dr. Jim Rosborg
Retired School Superintendent
Director, Master's in Education
McKendree University, IL

"The authors have provided a comprehensive resource for school leaders in planning, implementing, and evaluating school change that is focused on improving school programs and student achievement."

June Grivetti, EdD
University of St. Francis, IL

"The authors have provided an outstanding book on understanding the psychology and management of the change process. . . . I highly recommend this book as a resource for School Change Management."

Nick Osborne
Associate Professor
Eastern Illinois University

"Provocative and multifaceted . . . this text provides a basis from which educational leaders can elevate their understanding of change and school improvement by establishing real-world connections. This is truly a 'must-read' for any educational leader who is serious about school change."

Quintin Shepherd, PhD
School Superintendent
Illinois School District 69
Adjunct School Leadership Professor

"The in-depth and hands-on knowledge is clearly evident in *Leading School Change* and should serve as an invaluable tool to all educators."

Dr. Bradley A. Woodruff
Illinois State Board of Education
Manager, Secondary Education, Retired

"*Every School leader* must be an effective change driver. This book provides its readers with the necessary tools to impact positive change. Insight into the myriad of factors within the school setting and the skills that a school leader must have to be a successful change agent are provided.

"The reader is provided with a whole array of interventions that can be implemented. I especially liked the case studies that give the reader the opportunity to reflect on how they would utilize the many tools that are provided to them in this book. The book is a must for all school leaders."

Beverley H. Johns
Learning and Behavior Consultant and Adjunct Instructor
MacMurray College, IL

"For educators who want substantive and sustained success for their students, teachers and schools, this book provides a refreshing approach to the complex and often misunderstood process of change."

Dr. Lynn Bush, Associate Professor
Department of Educational Leadership and Development
Northeastern Illinois University, Chicago, IL

"The authors have put together a comprehensive work that will act as a road map to get you through change. *Leading School Change* addresses how change happens, the role of school leaders in dealing with change, and more importantly, how to be proactive in driving change. They provide a process for analyzing and evaluating data and give you a set of tools you can use to make a difference."

George Vukotich, PhD
Dean
College of Business
Concordia University Chicago
Author of *10 Steps to Successful Change Management*

"This book is a comprehensive and practical guide for any educator who desires current information on School Change Management. It is an outstanding book on understanding how to implement school change."

Mike Riggle, EdD
Superintendent
Glenbrook High School, District 225, IL

"No challenge facing school leaders is greater than that of leading through and for change. As both external and internal pressures create an ever-shifting educational landscape, the individual who can assess the obstacles, chart a course, and move teachers, students, and community forward to success is invaluable. *Leading School Change* will help aspiring leaders understand and develop the dispositions and skills needed for meeting these challenges."

Dr. Judith R. Merz
Retired School Superintendent
Editor, *The Delta Kappa Gamma Bulletin:*
International Journals for Professional Educators
Dissertation Advisor, Educational Leadership, Nova Southeastern University

"Educational leaders today are expected to be much more than good managers. They must understand and be able to bring about productive change in their schools. *Leading School Change* provides school leaders with important information they need to thoroughly understand all aspects of the school change process. It also offers practical strategies school leaders can use to help their schools become more efficient and effective."

Thomas A. Kersten, EdD
Professor Emeritus
Roosevelt University, Chicago, IL

"Leading School Change offers an easy to follow road map of how to make change in our American schools. The authors, who are practitioners as well as researchers, provide specific objectives with realistic strategies to make each of the school improvement changes easily implemented. There is no better resource available than this new publication packed with data-driven strategies."

Dr. T. Roger Taylor
President
Curriculum Design for Excellence
Oak Brook, IL

"With rich backgrounds in all levels of education and practical experience in leading change in various organizations, the authors provide a framework and road map based on sound research-based principles on the subject of educational change. Importantly, they provide useful resources, models, examples and practical strategies to help educational leaders address one of the most critical issues they will surely face: leading change in schools and districts."

Dr. Jay Linksman
Executive Director
Professional Development Alliance
Joliet, IL

"It is essential for the school leader to understand the journey of change and be convinced that change only comes about with a well-executed plan. Drs. Tomal, Trybus, and Schilling have been able to provide a road map for such organizational change that includes all of the stakeholders. Not only will the book be beneficial in an educational planning course, but also I can see it being used by current administrators to assist them in leading their schools and organizations."

Linda K. Lemasters, EdD
Associate Professor, Program Coordinator
Educational Administration and Policy Studies
The George Washington University

"The authors have succeeded in producing a practical guide on implementing the change process for new and experienced leaders that can be easily adapted to any school or district. Each chapter links sound management and educational principles to current changes impacting students, teachers, and administrators in Kindergarten through 12th grade schools. A valuable book to add to your leadership collection."

Dr. Patricia Ann Marcellino
Professor and Director
Educational Leadership Programs
Adelphi University, NY

"Much has been written about change recently, but most fall short when looking for a comprehensive treatment of the topic. In *Leading School Change: Maximizing Resources for School Improvement*, Dan Tomal, Marge Trybus, and Craig Schilling provide a complete package. I would recommend it to anyone who is looking for an up-to-date textbook on school change learning."

Fred C. Lunenburg
Merchant Professor of Education
Sam Houston State University, TX

"This exciting book has arrived at a time when change is accelerating, accountability is high, and resources are questionable. The authors blend research, theory, and tested practice to bring leaders innovative strategies and tools necessary to identify needed changes and to skillfully use data to monitor and evaluate the impact of school improvement initiatives. This is a book to help leaders become the change agents they dream about."

Dr. Bobb Darnell
National Professional Development Consultant
Achievement Strategies, Inc.
Lake Zurich, IL

"This book is relevant to all leaders who need to communicate change in their district or school. The explanations of the change process and the collaborative nature of successful practices are clear and useful and have a focus on serving the children."

Lynn Novak
Director of Curriculum
Westchester Public Schools
District 92 1/2, IL

"I recommend this research-based but very practical book as a great introduction to school leaders who are just beginning to think about managing change to experienced school leaders who will find it a comprehensive resource of strategies and interventions in dealing with the realities of change."

Dr. Donald Kachur
Professor Emeritus of Education
Illinois State University, IL

"Leading School Change: Maximizing Resources for School Improvement is a book with illuminating descriptions, discussions, case studies, frameworks, resources, leadership theories, exercises and references that can give focused energy to change team members to move forward on the journey of creating their school into a community of learners."

Paul Sims, PhD
Associate Professor, Educational Leadership
Concordia University
Chicago, IL

"This is a focused and comprehensive volume refining our understanding of school change and is replete with strategies for student achievement and more importantly their success. The practical strategies offered make this a fascinating book that will indeed provide a new and positive direction for school administration. It is an invaluable resource for educators no matter their level of experience."

Dr. Jason R. Mixon
Director
Doctoral Programs in Educational Leadership
Lamar University, TX

"On the international scene, education policy and change is a constant reality. A comprehensive guide on school evaluation and change is therefore very useful for teachers and policy makers in different parts of the world for reference purposes."

Dr. Sigrún Klara Hannesdóttir
Professor Emeritus
University of Iceland

"The value of this book includes the examination of school improvement in relation to the multitude of factors which should be considered when leading successful efforts. Student and school needs, data usage, research, change and leadership models, resources and budgets, and evaluation are considered along with case studies to assist current and future practitioners in school settings and preparation programs at the university level."

Dr. Barbara J. Phillips
Visiting Associate Professor
Concordia University
Chicago, IL

Leading School Change

OTHER TITLES BY DANIEL R. TOMAL, CRAIG A. SCHILLING, AND MARGARET A. TRYBUS

Leading School Change

Maximizing Resources for School Improvement

Daniel R. Tomal, Craig A. Schilling, and Margaret A. Trybus

ROWMAN & LITTLEFIELD EDUCATION

A division of
ROWMAN & LITTLEFIELD PUBLISHERS, INC.
Lanham • New York • Toronto • Plymouth, UK

Published by Rowman & Littlefield Education
A division of Rowman & Littlefield Publishers, Inc.
A wholly owned subsidiary of
The Rowman & Littlefield Publishing Group, Inc.
4501 Forbes Boulevard, Suite 200, Lanham, Maryland 20706

10 Thornbury Road, Plymouth PL6 7PP, United Kingdom

British Library Cataloguing in Publication Information Available

Library of Congress Cataloging-in-Publication Data Available

ISBN 978-1-4758-0329-7 (cloth : alk. paper)— ISBN 978-1-4758-0330-3 (pbk. :
alk. paper)— ISBN 978-1-4758-0331-0 (electronic)

♾™ The paper used in this publication meets the minimum requirements of
American National Standard for Information Sciences—Permanence of
Paper for Printed Library Materials, ANSI/NISO Z39.48-1992.

Printed in the United States of America

In appreciation to all the graduate faculty, administration, staff, and students at Concordia University Chicago who we have had the privilege to teach, learn, and work with in school leadership.

Contents

Foreword

Changing organizations in pursuit of improvement—even excellence—must be a collaborative effort facilitated by informed leadership. Leadership exhibits the characteristics of the expert—even gifted—conductor. That expertise will have been developed through the tangibles of education and experience but also through the exercise of intuition, vision, faith, and courage. This book provides the practitioner with the information, knowledge, and wisdom necessary to successfully manage and lead to and through change.

The authors provide the best of current thinking and practice relative to the data-informed realities of change management, like: finance, budget, student performance; resource allocation; and accountability systems. It also incorporates the best and current thinking relative to: change theory; leadership strategy; and professional development. Most importantly, the authors do a good job of addressing the most underestimated priority in effective change management—the Human Resource Development (HRD) issues. Personnel issues are often tragically undermanaged in the change process.

In short, this work is a state-of-the-art warehouse of change management knowledge. It is invaluable, because for change to bring benefit to and advance an organization to a higher level of excellence and operation that change must be driven by knowledge. If the goals include knowing: How and when to change? What kind of change is needed? How can change be effectively managed? And, how can we know that effort is producing the desired result? Then, this is the book to use as the reference!

Thomas P. Jandris, PhD
Vice President for Innovation
Dean of the College of Graduate and Innovative Programs
Concordia University Chicago
Founder and Managing Partner of EnterChange, Inc., Chicago, Illinois

Acknowledgments

Appreciation is extended to the many people who have assisted and worked with the authors. Special appreciation is given to the authors' students, colleagues, former business associates in the corporate world, Susan Webb for typing part of the manuscript, and Elaine Pierce for editing the manuscript. The authors would also like to recognize and extend appreciation to the many school districts where the authors have provided consulting such as the Chicago Public Schools, Bellwood School District 88, Cicero School District 99, Lake Central School Corporation, Proviso Township High Schools, West Chicago District 33, School District 131, Michigan City Township High Schools, Findlay Schools, Glenbrook High School District 225, West Northfield District 31, Lindop School District 92, Schiller Park District 81, Norridge School District 80, Rich Township High School District 227, Marquardt School District 15, Oswego Community Unit School District 308, Concordia University Chicago, Curriculum Leadership Development Network Illinois Association Supervision and Curriculum Development, and Lutheran Church Missouri Synod schools. Lastly, the authors would like to extend gratitude to the many people who endorsed this book and provided insight for this project.

Introduction

Leading school change is one of the most critical responsibilities of all school educators. This book has been written after years of study, research, and consulting in school leadership and change and evaluation initiatives. The models and strategies described in this book have been found to be successful in operating at multiple levels—department, unit, school building, and district.

Unlike other discourses on change, this book ties together change drivers and leadership with the use of resources for student achievement and school improvement. The book is unique as compared to other books on school change and evaluation in that it takes into account how resources (fiscal, facilities, and human resources) can be leveraged to improve student learning and achievement.

While primarily directed toward public schools, the strategies in this book can be effective for private elementary and secondary schools, and charter schools. The principles and strategies are practical and useful for any school educator or graduate student who desires to initiate and manage the school change process and improve student learning.

Chapter 1 begins by addressing the meaning and need for change in schools. The development of a *change framework* sets the concept of successful change by addressing individual, group, and organizational needs. School climate and culture are discussed through first- and second-order change examples. *Change drivers* at the federal, state, and local levels are explained in relationship to school improvement plans and reform. Ways to address change required for compliance by creating professional communities committed to change is discussed. A case study, thoughtful exercises, and discussion questions set the context for change through the lens of a school principal seeking school improvement.

The next chapter establishes the need for change leadership and presents ways to identify leaders in both formal and informal positions in organizational settings. The *Change Leadership Development Model* provides a process to define roles, qualities, skills, and ways to reward current and aspiring change leaders. Research-based leadership models are discussed within the change setting. The intrinsic and extrinsic motivation to become a change leader is reviewed. Lastly, insights on ways to strategically build a change team are presented as an important component in the change process. A case study from the perspective of a teacher leader provides exercises and discussion questions to create a successful school change leader.

The third chapter provides practical examples in conducting school-wide change such as the collaborative process intervention and the action research model. The use and application of interviews and surveys for obtaining information and collaborative involvement are given. Group and processing interventions are also clearly explained and several examples are provided to illustrate each of these techniques. Lastly, a comprehensive case study, exercises and questions, and references are provided.

Chapter 4 covers the use of research and statistics and data in change management. Topics understanding sources of data and research information, analyzing research data for threats to validity, understanding and analyzing statistical data, analyzing and using the *National Center for Education Statistics*, and interpreting national, state, and school performance data. There are also several examples of actual school data from various states such as New Jersey, California, and Illinois to provide concrete data and descriptions.

The next chapter introduces the *School Change Resource Implementation Model* and discusses each component. This is followed by a discussion of managing school resources, their relationship to student achievement, and their utilization to promote change. Lastly, there is a discussion of how to evaluate the effectiveness and efficiency of resources.

The last chapter discusses the *commonalities for change.* The drivers and factors that all districts face are covered from a resource management perspective. Change implementation strategies are also provided in dealing with future challenges. The chapter ends with a practical "how to" use the *School Change Resource Implementation Model* to execute change utilizing the concepts, drivers, change leadership, data analysis, and strategies discussed in the book.

FEATURES OF THE BOOK

This book is succinctly written and an easy read for graduate students and practicing educators. It is unique in that it provides many engaging examples that can be used by all educators. One feature of the book is the correlation of each chapter's objectives with professional organizational standards of the *National Council for Accreditation of Teacher Education* (NCATE), the Specialized Professional Association (SPA) of the *Educational Leadership Constituent Council* (ELCC), the *Interstate School Leaders Licensure Consortium* (ISLLC), and *National Standards for Quality Online Teaching* (NCOL) and *Southern Regional Education Board* (SREB).

Another valuable feature of the book is the incorporation of many leadership strategies, change processes, data and research, school change models, resources, and change evaluation techniques. The information is presented in a straightforward and practical manner. The topics in this book are useful for any school educator who desires to learn principles and strategies for initiating and evaluating school change and improving student performance.

Other features of this book include:

- practical examples of school change
- group interventions and techniques
- strategies for leading and managing the change effort
- models of school-wide change and small-scale and group change
- a comprehensive description of resources needed for change management
- practical strategies in helping stakeholders understand and implement change
- examples of interviewing and conducting change assessments
- a review of national, state, and district statistical data on school performance
- strategies in evaluating the change effort

Lastly this book also contains a rich source of educational and reference websites so that educators can apply the concepts for leading school change. The resources are the most up-to-date information on school change management.

Chapter One

The Nature of Change

OBJECTIVES

At the conclusion of this chapter you will be able to:

1. Understand the meaning of change and the impact on individual, groups, and organizations (ELCC 1.1, 1.2, 1.3, 1.4, 2.1, 3.1, 3.2, ISLLC 1, 2, 3).
2. Understand what drives change from federal, state, and school perspectives (ELCC 1.4, 2.2, 2.3, 3.1, 4.2, 6.1, 6.2, 6.3, ISLLC 1, 2, 3, 6).
3. Understand the role and importance of school climate and culture in bringing about successful change to improve student learning (ELCC 2.1, 2.2, 2.3, ISLLC 2).
4. Describe first- and second-order change, and its impact on schools, teachers, students, parents, and communities (ELCC 1.1, 1.2, 1.3, 1.4, 2.1, 2.2, 2.3, 2.4, 3.1, 3.2, 3.3, 4.1, 4.2, 4.3, 6.1, 6.2, ISLLC 1, 2, 3, 4, 6).
5. Describe the components of a school improvement plan related to the vision of learning that leads to success of all students (ELCC 1.1, 1.2, 1.3, 1.4, 1.5, 2.2, 2.3, 2.4, ISLLC 1, 2, 3).
6. Explain the difference between compliance and commitment to change (ELCC 6.1, 6.2, 6.3, ISLLC 6).

THE MEANING AND NEED FOR CHANGE

Schools, like many organizations, have to adjust to constant change and face daunting challenges inherent in the process of change. School change can be seen as a probable element that will always exist and is a nonnegotiable part of education systems. Changes in federal, state, and local requirements, student populations, curriculum, instruction, assessment, and faculty and school leadership are just a few of the areas that will always exist in schools. Because of these realities, change agents will be required to develop the knowledge, skills, and leadership dispositions to understand the concept of school change.

This change is essential in order to effectively manage, lead, and improve schools. Involvement by all stakeholders at multiple levels of engagement such as school board members, administrators, teachers, staff members, parents and community members, and students is needed for the change process. Change agents need the collaboration of stakeholders to respond to change and make meaning of it. Essentially schools will move forward or backward, but there is no standing still.

Since change is so prevalent in schools, educators often don't analyze what helps *make meaning* or sets the context for the work inherent in the change process. Fullan (2007) points out that regardless if the change is imposed or voluntary a sense of loss and anxiety is created simply because it is a new experience that will cause a reaction. These reactions can be dealt with more effectively if people can attach "personal meaning to the experiences" in a way that is individualized yet collectively understood as needed for the organization to improve (Fullan, 2007; Stivers & Cramer, 2009).

Teachers typically *make meaning* through their experiences in and outside the classroom. If they perceive the change as related to what they have done or can do in the classroom, then *making meaning* may be understandable and doable. On the other hand, if the perception of the change is unreasonable, or requires additional knowledge, skills, and training that are not readily available or obtainable, then *making meaning* will be difficult and perhaps unlikely.

Particularly with imposed change, levels of uncertainty and potential internal struggle will present barriers to individual *meaning making*. The change agent must communicate in such a way that helps people understand that the change initiative will occur for individual and organizational benefit. When the change is explained as a way to bring improvement to the school and ultimately student learning, acceptance is more likely to occur.

Administrators, as well, often struggle *making meaning* of change when it is imposed through federal, state, and local policies. Uncertain as to the motives or the underlying factors that precipitate the requirement to change, administrative anxiety may permeate the school even if unintentional. These factors are often accountability driven, and are the result of policy decisions that local administrators have little if any involvement in making.

At the federal and state level, school boards are also driven to create policies that local administrators must respond to and implement with minimal, if any, clarity on how to explain and help teachers and parents understand the need and urgency of the change. When the implications of the change at the school level are not clear, confusion and resistance may result.

Parents may struggle with *making meaning* of change since they view it through the lens of impact on their own child. This is certainly understandable since parents are their child's advocates; however, changes that might occur to address the needs of all children at a particular grade level, and in a specific school setting, may not be appropriate for that parent's child.

If parents don't see the need for change that will help their own child, they may be reluctant to support the change. This may be the result of policy mandates at the federal level intended for whole school change, or it could be change at the local level that grew out of research or best practices that offer school-wide improvement.

Staff members are also vital to support school-level change, and the need to *make meaning* of it in order to help the day-to-day operations and management. When change results in alterations to working conditions, individual job satisfaction and engagement may also change. This can be positive when the situation shows greater engagement and benefit to the individual or, conversely, negative if fears and anxiety as to the value and worth of the individual to the organization seems at risk.

The question as to the appropriateness of the change, from the perspectives of administrators, teachers, staff members, and parents will determine the extent of understanding why the change is occurring at the local school-community level. Individual and group processes in *making meaning* can quickly become a gauge as to the success or failure of the initiative. To help foster understanding, individuals need to realize that, in most cases, the school as an organization is driving change in order to improve, grow, and meet increasing demands.

If the change agent develops a framework that distinguishes between individual needs, versus organizational needs, then the realization of the complexities of change can be better dealt with. This framework suggests that individual and various group needs surrounding change must be addressed at the same time the organizational needs are being studied and acted upon.

Figure 1.1.   Change Framework

Figure 1.1 illustrates a framework that sets the context for change. The interrelatedness of three levels of need is essential to consider during the planning and implementation stages. The complexity of change impacts individuals, groups, and school organizations, which requires differentiated approaches in dealing with the change at all three levels.

Individual Needs

The *individual needs* indicated in the *Change Framework* address the psychological aspects of change that cannot be predicted. What may be acceptable change for one person may not be to another, even if both individuals work in the same organization. This is always a tricky situation for the change agent.

Individual change may be impossible to understand simply because people accept or resist change based on a myriad of factors, many of which are beyond the control of the school organization. Nevertheless, some basic understanding of human behavior can help the change agent manage individual differences, and adjust approaches with sensitivity to meeting individual needs.

When individuals experience change they may resist it or embrace it depending on if they see the potential for growth versus loss (Evans, 1996; Senge, 1999). Knowing that the environment will change, the individual can interpret opportunities for *personal and professional growth* and improvement if the change brings about his or her own learning and job enhancement.

This strategy works well for individual teachers who realize that what they are doing in the classroom is not working, and they are committed to help all students learn. It also presents an opportunity for people to gain new skills that might help them move up the career ladder.

Teachers, by profession, are lifelong learners, so the opportunity to present *change as growth* should be clearly communicated, discussed, and planned by the change agent (Evans, 1996).

This can take the form of clearly defined professional development associated with the needed change, as well as the recognition for those willing risk takers, who demonstrate changes in practices that align with the change initiative. Individual professional growth needs to be seen as progress toward embracing change, and championed by the change agent personally, publically, and professionally.

There is a dual purpose that is served when individual growth is recognized and celebrated. This makes a clear statement that change (and risk taking) is part of the cultural norms of the school. Change is also dependent on career stages since a beginning, midcareer, or close-to-retirement teacher will perceive the needs for growth differently.

Helping each teacher feel challenged yet supported through the change initiative maximizes the opportunities for buy-in and ownership. Change agents need to strategically provide opportunities to create personal and professional growth associated with change. This is the foundation of initiating change management.

When schools desperately need to improve, they may ignore the importance of identifying individual needs and overlook the fact that human beings can quickly become fearful of change. Being aware that teacher performance may be beyond the knowledge and skills required to implement the change focuses on individual needs rather than an assumption of lack of interest to change.

When individuals appear vulnerable to change they exhibit feelings of *change as loss* (Evans 1996). They feel threatened because their environment may be altered for reasons that are not clearly understood. Individual comfort levels without a clear rationale as to what is driving the change, and how the decision to change was made, may be upsetting. This is symptomatic of poor communication, which leads to confusion.

Since teachers face so many challenges within the classroom, changing what might be part of their teaching routine and habits requires rethinking about their performance, creating a sense of fear. Without sensitivity to individual needs, and the realization that as human beings maintaining the status quo is easier than relearning, change agents often are seen as insensitive to acknowledging how hard it is for individuals to change professionally, and perhaps personally.

If change agents can demonstrate insight and encouragement that meets individual needs, a shift from dreading change to having confidence to change can hopefully begin to surface (Stivers & Cramer, 2009). Relationship building is critical so that positive interactions and problem solving can shift feelings of loss to feelings of growth (Fullan, 2007).

The influence of positive relationships and the perception that the change agent takes into account individual needs and opportunities for growth is vital for *change as growth*. When individuals reframe negative feelings of change to positive feelings of growth, the attitudes and emotions surrounding change can help preserve individual strengths and build on them, at the same time meeting organizational needs.

Another factor to consider when dealing with individuals' need to cope and engage in change is the *mental model* that influences their beliefs and behaviors (Senge, 2006; Senge et al., 1994). *Mental models* are very powerful forces that influence the perception of *change as loss or growth*, since they develop through individual experiences and beliefs. *Mental models* may account for individual openness to change, interpersonal reactions to change, and unconscious behaviors that develop as a result of change.

Change agents must develop the skills that (1) recognize individual feelings of *change as loss, and change as growth* embedded in *mental models;* (2) communicate with clarity the needs of the organization in relationship to individual *personal and professional growth*; and (3) build relationships that foster trust and understanding that individual needs are being considered during times of organizational change.

Addressing individual needs will help build *resiliency* to face the complexity of understanding the need for change and the speed with which it needs to occur (Conner, 1993). When individuals are *resilient,* their tolerance for the need and ambiguity of change can be dealt with and they see themselves not as the victims of change, but the beneficiaries of change.

The purpose of addressing individual needs related to change is to help all stakeholders be successful so that the organization can reap the benefits. At the same time, individuals who become enabled to contribute to the change create ownership that spreads to others. Since individuals are members of groups in formal and informal settings, consideration for group needs is also part of the *Change Framework* (see figure 1.1).

Change agents who understand and lead groups within schools demonstrate awareness of the importance of group support. They need to be sensitive in creating a culture and climate that are supportive to change. People will be more receptive to embracing change when these collaborative and environmental aspects are taken into consideration.

Group Needs

Change agents not only need to be sensitive to individual needs, but also need to be concerned with addressing *group needs*. There are two types of groups in organizations: *formal* and *informal*. Successful school change is dependent on groups to provide the infrastructure necessary for successful planning, implementing, and sustaining the change.

Formal groups within school settings are structured at department, grade, and course levels. They can also be created as specialized teams to address school improvement in curricular, instructional, and assessment programs.

Specialized teams may also be formed to address student needs, not only in academic areas but behavioral and social as well. *Formal* groups are typically appointed since members are chosen based on specific skills, experience, and knowledge. They exist for particular reasons related to job responsibilities and often complete designed tasks related to organizational needs.

Informal groups also exist in school settings. An example of this may be new or veteran teacher groups, mentor groups, lunch groups, or social groups of individuals who gravitate toward each other in informal ways that help meet individual needs of belonging. This type of group formation is typically voluntary and may not have specifically defined roles within the school. By virtue of their existence, they become part of the school culture and may be influential in the change process.

Formal and *informal* groups also exist at parent and community levels often seen through parent and teacher organizations, subcommittees of boards of education, volunteer groups, strategic planning groups, and task forces designed for a specific purpose that interrelates to change. Community groups are also considerations since they can coalesce with forces that may impact the governance of the school.

Groups that converge within the organization are very powerful in supporting and challenging the need to change and how to implement it. It is for this reason that cultivating and addressing group needs is part of the *Change Framework*. Group needs require distinctive strategies since they are essential in establishing the teamwork that supports and builds a culture for change in schools.

The change agent is instrumental in helping groups accept and foster a *shared purpose* for change. This goes back to the understanding of the need to change, especially bringing about growth and improvement at the individual and organizational level. When groups have a sense of *shared purpose*, they help define roles, responsibilities, and collective action that makes change happen.

The element of shared purpose also exhibits shared ownership to assist in the change process in ways that no individual can succeed in accomplishing alone. This shifts the burden to bring about change from the individual to the group. This is essential and is called *operationalizing* the change initiative.

Fueled by team energy and development, teams of experts, teams of risk takers, and teams of committed individuals work to establish *collegiality*. *Collegiality* supports collaboration that is mindful of individual needs, and at the same time creates synergy to make the change initiative happen. Collegiality helps groups reach consensus and can establish the climate to bring disparaging points of view together. When divergent thinking complements the vision for the change, the group creates the *shared purpose* change agents need to be successful.

Lack of *collegiality* can lead to faulty assumptions and pressures that get in the way of positive change. This can be the result of limited or incorrect information, group pressure, lack of trust, and beliefs that don't align with the vision for change. Inefficient decision making and the emergence of *balkanized groups* where loyalties prevent acceptance to innovation and change are issues for the change agent to contend with.

Balkanized groups are isolated, difficult to convert to *shared purpose*, and can even result in hostility that derails change. Members of these *balkanized groups* can impact the organizational culture in negative ways, requiring the change agent to be conscious of their existence while strategizing ways to deal with them.

These negative factors often take the form of group loyalties that are based on fear, lack of trust, and inaccurate information. Without focus on the influence of *balkanized groups* and without efforts to foster positive interaction with them, they will become a barrier to change.

Developing groups to become *collaborative cultures*, where trust and support for change occurs, is a constant but necessary challenge in schools. Successful implementation of change depends on *collaborative cultures*. Group and organizational needs require collaboration rather than isolation of teams of individuals. Through interdependence, groups become stronger since they recognize each and every individual's talents are needed for collaborative change.

Rather than working in "silos," *collaborative cultures* foster and encourage peer interaction. When collaboration is recognized and celebrated as a result of positive change, the culture grows and accepts change that becomes part of the school climate.

School climate is based on perceptions about how people feel and reflects the attitudes of groups (Gruenert, 2008). *School climate* impacts all stakeholders, especially teachers and students. "How students, teachers, and staff feel about their school climate underlies individual attitudes, behaviors, and group norms" (Loukas, 2007, p. 1).

There is no doubt that a positive *school climate* can leverage *school culture* to determine if improvement is possible. *School climate* is part of the spirit of the organization where the morale and the perception to deal with challenges can result in a strong or negative *culture*. This concept is critical in linking the concepts to managing change within the organization.

When the climate is flexible the culture may move more quickly to embrace change. When the climate is negative then the *culture* of the school transmits feelings of uncertainty and potential resistance to change. This can essentially undermine the change initiative even with the greatest change management plan.

Both school culture and climate influence groups to accept change based on the vision of the school and the need to improve. When groups help establish a *positive school climate*, an improved *school culture* is the favorable outcome. The perspectives, frames of mind, and collective responsibility to change are healthy and proactive in *positive school climates*.

School climate shapes *school culture* and can help perceptions of change related to physical, instructional, and social elements that may be needed for school improvement. School climate helps groups become cohesive and connected to deal with change. When *school climate* supports a *culture* of change, teachers and students are more willing to change since this becomes an organization norm. Excitement, opportunity, and the discovery of change can lead to innovation and improvement.

Change agents need to develop the skills necessary to address group needs including (1) creating a *shared purpose* for the need to change; (2) understanding the impact of positive and negative group behaviors on *collegiality*; and (3) establishing a *culture* and *climate* that maximizes successful change in schools. Since change is part of the school improvement process, eliciting groups of stakeholders to create the *climate* and *culture* necessary to develop quality teaching and learning will maximize results to improve student achievement.

Organizational Needs

Like individual and group needs, there are unique *organizational needs*. When change occurs in organizations, a strategic call to action needs to be clearly communicated. This requires clear and honest communication as to the state the organization is currently in and where it needs to go to continuously improve.

School improvement initiatives significantly drive change; however, organizational needs to improve student achievement are also dependent on availability of school resources which have to be carefully assessed in order to provide the support needed for school improvement. The amount and depth of change is a consideration for the change agent since some change may be incremental and short term, whereas more organization systemic needs will require deeper change that will take more time and insight.

First- and Second-Order Change

Assessing organizational needs will determine the extent and degree to which the organization must change. This change may begin with *first-order* or surface change, which will impact selected departments or components within the organization. For example, *first-order change* may be a particular program or event that involves a change in an existing practice in some part of the organization, but not the whole organization.

This might be changes in report card pickup, a specific reading program, involvement of school volunteers for an event, or a specific classroom change. *First-order change* may be seen as incremental change, and could lead to more systemic or *second-order* change but does not initially involve the entire school system (Stivers & Cramer, 2009).

Organizations need to consider *first-order change* that may take the form of *pilot projects*, which can be analyzed and studied. This strategy is worth considering since *pilot projects* that result in positive outcomes can help address organizational needs but not be disruptive to the entire school system.

Typically, *pilot projects* may be conducted internally but evaluated externally, especially if grant related. Small-scale classroom or program projects allow for experimentation before full adoption occurs. *First-order change* that can demonstrate successful outcomes may over time lead to *second-order change*, which will impact more components of the organization.

Grant programs often address organizational needs based on school improvement and innovation and require both *first-* and *second-order change*. Grant revenue comes from external sources which are either compensatory or competitive. Compensatory grants are federally funded and typically serve special populations of students such as at-risk, special education, bilingual, and migrant students. These grants target students who need special services that the federal government mandates through policy and state legislation.

Compensatory services are grant funded because they often extend beyond the regular school day or they alter the school day in such a way as to require additional resources. Examples of compensatory grant funding include the Title programs, which are based on local school district needs. Data including free and reduced lunch counts, state test scores, and demographics drive the opportunity for school districts to qualify for compensatory grants.

Small-scale grants, which are usually competitively funded, are also examples of *first-order change* since they require new or expanded program development. Competitive grants help inspire creativity and innovation to address organizational needs in new and varied ways. For example, competitive grants may be state funded to expand on school improvement initiatives. Other opportunities may be explored through locally funded competitive grants which are created by professional organizations that create opportunities for targeted funding in specific areas.

For example, projects in visual and performing arts, multiliteracies, gifted or at-risk programs, and career and technical education may start small, involving a limited number of teachers and students to encourage experimentation. Competitive grants that reward innovations to change are often implemented through *first-order change pilot projects,* which are studied, evaluated, and can lead to successful change.

Over time, *pilot projects* may add value by including additional student and teacher populations within the school. This level of change addresses organizational needs without having a major impact on the organization since *pilot projects* may address only one segment of the school population or programs. Creative problem solving and small-scale change that addresses targeted populations of students and specific programs offer promise to change beliefs and practices that can ultimately lead to whole school *second-order* change.

Second-order change influences the norms and values within the school culture. The merits of change at this level are predicated on changing beliefs and practices on a large scale within the entire organization. For example, a move to block scheduling, small schools, career academies, redistricting, or changes to the discipline policy will require long-term change that impacts school norms, relationships, and even school structures for management and leadership.

Second-order change involves all stakeholders in addressing the organizational needs so that the school will be able to adjust to the increasing needs of education in the twenty-first century. More specifically needs at the school level that impact students, families, and communities may be at the core of second-order change and bring needed improvement.

Professional Learning Communities

Another consideration related to organizational needs is the development of *professional learning communities.* DuFour (2004) states, " People use this term to describe every imaginable combination of individual with an interest in education—a grade-level teaching team, a school committee, a high school department, an entire school district, a state department of education, a national professional organization, and so on" (p. 1).

Professional learning communities address organizational needs since they are designed around three major tenets related to school improvement. These include: (1) ensuring students are learning, which shifts organizational needs from a focus on teaching to a focus on learning; (2) creating structures to develop a collaborative culture; and (3) focusing on results to measure meeting organizational goals (DuFour, 2004).

These tenets help move the school forward to improve by setting expectations that become school-wide priorities, and establish a culture that supports collaboration. Communities of teachers working together ends the isolation that occurs when individuals are not aware or engaged in meeting organizational needs.

The design of strategies through coordinated efforts in professional learning communities can create a climate of working together in a positive school culture that aligns individuals with the mission and vision of change. With collaborative conversations—and a clearly defined focus on organizational needs to improve teaching and learning—individuals and identified groups can align efforts that will bring about successful school change.

When change agents address organizational needs they need to take into account (1) the degree of change needed for *first order* or *second order*, determined by assessing the current situation; (2) consider compensatory and competitive *grants* and *pilot projects* as a way to experiment with change strategies that lead to measurable outcomes; and (3) establish *professional learning communities* where stakeholders are organized to work together in collaboration, providing a vehicle for engagement in meeting the needs of the organization.

When it comes to the hard work of change, teachers, administrators, parents, and community representatives are all members of groups of individuals who will influence the change initiative and ultimately have a shared commitment to make it happen. By carefully examining the need for change through the lens of individuals, groups, and ultimately the organization, the change agent can consider all possibilities for involvement and engagement to meet these collective needs.

When needs are met, individual and group efficacy turn beliefs into support for change. Even though the pathway to actualize the change might not yet be clear, the change agent should be able to call on support from others and not be alone in the change process.

CHANGE DRIVERS: FEDERAL, STATE, AND SCHOOL LEVELS

School change can often be hard because the impetus comes from so many directions. It is a force that oftentimes is unanticipated due to the school

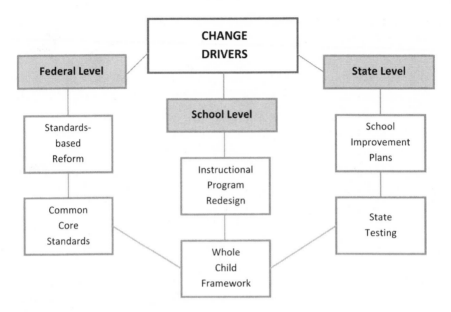

Figure 1.2.   School Change Drivers

community's response to changing conditions that exist within the school and outside in the larger educational arena. These conditions might be cultural or environmental and may exist within society. School change is reflective of pressures to address student achievement and educational reform including school restructuring, and policy changes result in accountability to show measurable improvement.

Different reform efforts are driven by federal and state mandates that trickle down to schools and classrooms. Imagine a funnel where change gets poured into the top (federal government) and drives the needs and requirement to change, although not completely understood and accepted. As the change flows through the funnel (state level), it becomes a little clearer but adds more complexity due to more involvement of stakeholders and policy makers who try to make rules and regulations more explicit on how the change will eventually be implemented.

Moving down the funnel, the change mixes with state and federal messaging so that impact on local school needs begins to take form. Local school leaders then start figuring out how to take action to deal with the change that is coming down the funnel from two directions, and add to the mix a third direction which includes the local flavor which hopefully aligns with identified needs.

As the change moves down the funnel, it impacts the classroom, where teachers and students will have to analyze it and take action on it. What flows from the funnel is now tainted with federal, state, local school, and classroom interpretations. These interpretations drive change in response to school reform and restructuring which are complex due to the growing pressures that lobby for attention to make change happen.

Whether you agree or disagree, legislation, federal policies, and mandates are change drivers that have to be contended with in schools. Because of the complexity of these requirements, they can be misunderstood and confusing, requiring the change agent to pay particular attention to the details of accountability and compliance that drives local school change.

Federal Change Drivers

An example of change at the federal level is the seminal National Commission report (1983) *A Nation at Risk: The Imperative for Educational Reform.* With the federal government's growing concern that American schools were failing at the time, especially in addressing the national need to create a workforce, this report triggered many educational reforms that still exist today. Schools were seen as mediocre, test scores were dropping, and the quality of teaching and learning was questioned, especially in comparison to other countries. As a result, schools were headed for large-scale *second-order change.*

This report involved raising standards for all students, and resulted in the *standards-based reform* movement which trickled down to states causing systemic change in curriculum and instruction (Duke, 2004). *Standards-based reform* became the centerpiece of another federal change driver, *No Child Left Behind Act of 2001 (NCLB),* which grew out of legislation with the passage of the *Improving America's School Act of 1994 (IASA)* (Jorgensen & Hoffman, 2003).

National data indicated that many students were at risk due to indicators of illiteracy, especially among minority youth, declining test scores in reading and mathematics, and declining graduation rates. States and school districts were charged with meeting challenging content standards especially in reading and mathematics with the intent that *all children* would meet standards by 2014. This federal change required a shift to high-stakes testing, which states were charged with creating and managing.

High-stakes testing continues to be used as a way to determine results of meeting federal requirements at the district and school level, creating sanctions and penalties if the results don't indicate expected improvement results. Since the NCLB regulations have become increasingly stringent on states and schools, accountability has become the change driver to improve teaching and learning. As federal mandates drive educational reform, states are impacted and often want flexibility through waivers in order to interpret the mandates and provide support to schools during this large-scale change effort (see chapter 5).

State Change Drivers

State departments of education are faced with the trickle-down effect which addresses all children, including special populations of children. Federal mandates impact state policies in addressing areas such as: special education, gifted education, bilingual and English language learners, low-income children, and early childhood education, to name a few.

States become change drivers to schools with increasing requirements for *school improvement* which may vary slightly from state to state. Essentially school improvement plans have the same structure of looking at what is taught, how it is taught, and how it is measured related to the mission, vision, and core beliefs of the school district. When this process involves all stakeholders at the local level, federal mandates are addressed in alignment with identified school needs.

School improvement planning and implementation is one form of driving change since it is a comprehensive approach to change and needs to be embedded in the school culture. *School improvement* planning and implementation aligns with the Change Framework (figure 1.1) in that it assesses the organization's needs through extensive data collection and analysis to indicate areas in need of improvement, and then seeks individuals and groups to address changes in teaching and learning.

School Improvement

State departments of education typically provide templates for school improvement planning, since the document is required by law and is part of compliance monitoring. *School improvement plans* are approved by the state and local boards of education. They are monitored by the state since they hold schools accountable and compliant to address state standards and assessments for *all* children. Student data are analyzed for all subgroups of students by: English language learners, gender, special education, racial and ethnic groups, and socioeconomic levels. For example, *school improvement plans* include the following components:

1. *Data and Analysis; Identification of Key Factors*—typically from the school report card, indicating areas of strengths and weakness, and causes of low student performance.
2. *Mission, Vision, and Core Values*—the development, articulation, implementation, and stewardship of who we are, why we exist, where we are going, and who/what is important.
3. *Action Plan: Clarity of Objectives*—measurable indicators that address the needed areas for improvement that will be driving improvement typically over a two-year period.
4. *Action Plan: Alignment of Strategies and Activities*—ways to improve student outcomes, including professional development for teachers and parental involvement.
5. *Monitoring*—indication of who internally will be responsible for oversight of the plan and continuous monitoring of its progress through data collection and analysis.
6. *Methods of Plan Development, Review, and Implementation*—addresses parent notification of the plan, stakeholder involvement, peer review, and a teacher mentoring process to ensure appropriate training.
7. *District and State Responsibilities*—ensure internal and external support and an understanding of corrective action and restructuring options if needed.
8. *School Support Team and Board Action*—identification of the members and indication of their expertise to support the plan; approval of the local board of education.

(Adapted from Illinois State Board of Education, School Improvement Monitoring Prompt, 2010; School Improvement Plan template, State of Michigan)

School Change Drivers

State compliance results in continuous school improvement efforts that drive change in schools. School change that has its genesis in *state and federal mandates* often requires *second-order change* in resources, organizational structure, and local policies and procedures for implementing the school improvement plan. This drives change at the classroom level since this is where the impact on teaching and learning occurs.

Evidence of *school-based change* can be seen in changes to the instructional program designed to develop quality teaching that will improve student achievement. With the development of the *Common Core State Standards*, school-based instructional programs are in the midst of standards alignment, curriculum mapping, and evaluating the relevance of what is currently being taught. According to the Common Core State Standards Initiative (2012):

> *The Common Core State Standards* provide a consistent, clear understanding of what students are expected to learn, so teachers and parents know what they need to do to help them. The standards are designed to be robust and relevant to the real world, reflecting the knowledge and skills that our young people need for success in college and careers. (Common Core State Standards, 2012)

The *Common Core State Standards* will not only drive changes to "what" is taught, but also "how" content will be taught. Changes to instructional delivery methods will require teachers to review problem solving and higher-order thinking strategies, rather than teach to lower-level knowledge and recall skills. This will require ongoing professional development to train teachers in curriculum mapping and standards alignment.

Research-based strategies will be required to meet the demands of the new *Common Core State Standards*. Classroom lessons will need to be evaluated, redesigned, and reevaluated so that changes in student learning will reach desired outcomes. Formative and summative assessment plans will need to be not only at the classroom level, but also at the school level to align with expected state assessments. Transitioning to this new paradigm will require school-level professional development, so that teachers will be equipped with the skills needed to change practice.

School-level change has to keep focused on student needs. In addition to academic needs related to social, emotional, and behavior issues, components of student growth and development need to be assessed for possible change initiatives. For example, programs dealing with student behavior, attendance, motivation, character education, and drug and alcohol prevention can also be part of school change. Social and emotional issues that prevent students from successfully learning need to be addressed. This is particularly crucial where parental involvement is lacking and family structures are not supporting the child's needs.

Outside school factors within communities may also require the creation of school and community partnerships. When teachers, school, parents, and communities share a common vision for school improvement and share resources and expertise, changing school environments may need to be developed that support the needs of the *whole child*.

An example of school-wide change can be found in the *whole child* approach, which according to the *Association of Supervision and Curriculum Development* (ASCD) "ensures that each student is healthy, safe, engaged, supported, and challenged, sets the standard for comprehensive, sustainable school improvement and provides for long-term student success." The tenants of the whole child can help guide school change, and provide a framework to support a multifaceted approach to improving student learning.

Change drivers, as illustrated in figure 1.2, exist at the federal, state, and local levels. The change agent has to sort out these drivers in order to determine the urgency of change and the scale of change (*first- or second-order*). The change agent also needs to develop knowledge and understanding of federal and state policies; research-based strategies to improve curriculum, instruction, and assessment; and a holistic understanding of the needs of the *whole child*.

When *school improvement* drives change that is focused on the needs of students in classrooms, teachers who have to change practice, parents who need to be involved, and communities who partner with schools, the change process can lead to tangible and intangible results that are positive and rewarding.

COMPLIANCE VERSUS COMMITMENT TO CHANGE

Compliance drives change, but mandated change is often resisted. At times when multiple mandates permeate schools, change agents are left to determine the sense of urgency and prioritize initiatives. People also have to have sufficient urgency to become energized to bring about successful change (Kotter, 2002). Urgency should be seen as a motivator that encourages people to get involved in the change, which is hard to do when compliance looms. With required compliance to federal and state mandates, accountability for results is a reality.

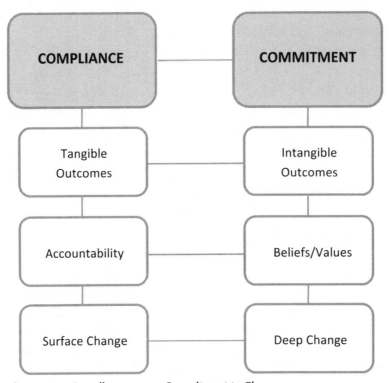

Figure 1.3. Compliance versus Commitment to Change

Compliance coupled with accountability creates fear and confusion within the organization if not carefully and strategically addressed. Compliance can be seen as an opportunity that requires a shift from fear to innovation. Innovation takes creativity and the ability to take risks that hold promise for improvement. It is for this reason that the change agent needs to work toward shifting change from compliance to commitment. Figure 1.3 illustrates counterbalancing change from compliance to commitment.

Educational compliance is the result of legislation and policy that mandates schools and individuals to change in order to exist. Improved student achievement is at the core of compliance, with measurable outcomes the indicator. Statewide assessment systems have changed the way schools operate instructional programs, since standardized tests determine not only student learning, but program evaluation and school improvement targets.

External sets of standards ensure schools focus student and teacher performance in meeting specific indicators that are measurable. Standards-based curricular programs, mandated teacher evaluation methods, and school report cards have changed the landscape of school improvement. This has resulted in the assessment and reporting of student learning outcomes which is conducted by states and reported to the public on an annual basis.

In order to be compliant, schools are rated based on the annual state assessment which can cause fear and threats to schools and teachers. Change based on these compliant measures is often reactionary and does require tactics and resources for quick solutions designed to show immediate improvement.

School compliance also addresses state requirements for teacher and administrator certification and federal requirements to be NCLB Highly Qualified. Teachers need to be certified in specific content areas (science, mathematics, physical education, language arts, fine arts, etc.) and in addition may need added training in specialized areas. For example, endorsements in special areas such as: grade levels (pre–K, elementary, middle, high school), special education, bilingual/English language learners, and reading also require additional teacher coursework.

National board teacher and principal certification are also options with specific requirements. When certification and endorsements change, teachers are threatened and fearful for their jobs. Schools may also find shortages in finding teachers who meet these specific requirements. This dilemma drives compliant change due to the pressure at both the individual and organizational level.

Requirements related to class sizes in specialized areas, certain groupings of students, and mandated programs also impact school compliance and are often written into law. These imposed change requirements may require additional resources which may be difficult for the school to obtain. The costs of change may not be acknowledged or funded, resulting in strain on the school and community.

Change that occurs due to compliance requires *tangible outcomes*. This is critical in order to meet accountability requirements and demonstrate compliance. For example, school improvement plans, school and individual student test scores, teacher evaluation procedures, professional development plans, minutes from planning meetings, and action research projects must lead to *tangible outcomes* that are measurable.

Data associated with this type of change can be collected, analyzed, and used to show what, how, and why change occurred. *Tangible outcomes* present a very clear understanding of the response to change which results in *school improvement* and the process to meet federal and state mandates. Evidence of compliance-driven change is not an option, but rather a requirement that change-agent leaders need to know, understand, and strategically deliver.

The paradox of this type of change is that it may be *surface change* and *first order* which does not change beliefs or values, and may not lead to the *commitment to change*, which is a component of *second-order* systemic change. The formal structure of compliance sometimes overlooks the context of change within the *culture* of the school. Mandates matter and are part of the accountability world of schools; however, administrators, teachers, students, and parents will have to change practices and behaviors and perhaps even the school vision to commit to change for improvement.

Commitment to change as illustrated in figure 1.3 requires *deep change* beyond the management of the change process. *Deep change* realizes that the psychological aspect inherent in people changing for the sake of the organization requires *making meaning* of change in order to commit to it. *Deep change* takes into account the fact that any lasting change will derail if commitment doesn't develop in the planning, implementation, and evaluation of change. Attention to rules and roles cannot usurp attention to systems of values and beliefs that lead to *deep change*.

Commitment building is dependent on *culture* building. *School culture* helps reframe *compliance* into a process of improvement that is seen to be in the best interest of the school. *Commitment* will develop if change is seen as possible and needed for the good of the school and the students who deserve a quality education. *Commitment* is dependent on a clear sense of purpose that engages people in shared goals for improvement.

Relationship building is also a positive *intangible outcome* as a result of stakeholder commitment. This can lead to increased job satisfaction since relationships of trust lead to team building that shares both the burden and the success of change. Working together with groups within the school, the change-agent leader acknowledges that even a committed individual cannot produce school change without the dedication and commitment of others.

Moving from *compliance* to *commitment* results in *intangible outcomes* that include faculty willingness to take risks, innovative thinking for experimentation, and motivation to change. An improved *school culture* where teachers collaborate and share instructional strategies that have the potential to improve student learning is evident. Increased volunteerism and accepting roles required for school improvement in addition to classroom teaching becomes a school norm.

Compliance is an opportunity to evaluate what is working and not working in the school system, and can change negative assumptions derived from mandates into possibilities. Actions to improve teaching and learning hold promise that can be endured. Openness to the challenges of change, the convening of all stakeholders to create the change, and the celebration of change when it occurs is an intangible outcome the change agent needs to strategically orchestrate. Despite the elusiveness of change, and the uncertainty of positive measurable outcomes, a *commitment* to stay on course for change is required to make change work.

The change agent needs to be aware of *compliance versus commitment* to change. Mandated or voluntary change can often be misunderstood, misinterpreted, and miscommunicated. Without this understanding of what is driving the change, people will struggle to *make meaning* of it on a personal and professional level. The result is often a failed change initiative.

Therefore, change agents must realize how change is perceived. Developing the skills to move stakeholders from compliance to commitment within the organization is the role of the change agent. Perceptions of change determine the impetus for the change process and will affect the attitudes and the results of how schools and the people within them improve.

SUMMARY

It is essential for schools to understand the meaning of change in order to make it happen. Interpreting change with respect for individual, group, and organizational needs leads to successful change. The change agent needs to be skilled in understanding and interpreting these three components of the *Change Framework* in order to maximize change leading to school improvement.

Individual needs include opportunities for personal and professional growth so that investment in the change process is seen as rewarding. This requires accepting *change as growth* rather than *change as loss*. Individuals also have to contend with their *mental models* of change based on past experiences that may contribute or conflict with school change. Individuals need to be resilient to accept and embrace school change.

Group needs are essential in developing a shared purpose for change that leads to collegiality. Groups can be created formally or develop informally. Collegiality is needed since change cannot be accomplished successfully without teamwork and a collaborative school culture. The change agent is a catalyst to develop a school culture where trust and support for change becomes the norm. School climate impacts school culture in dealing with stakeholder morale and the perceptions of change.

Organizational needs include *first- and second-order change* that determines the amount and type of change. Pilot projects are often good ways to field-test first-order change before systemic second-order change occurs. Grant projects often provide opportunities for both small- and large-scale change. Professional learning communities help organizations organize teams of teachers to address school improvement needs and foster collaboration and shared decision making about change.

The change agent needs to determine what drives change at federal, state, and local levels. The intensity of these drivers impacts school improvement in the areas of curriculum, instruction, and assessment. The resources to accomplish improvement include human and financial resources and are a critical consideration to respond to change mandates.

Change drivers include compliance mandates that require the commitment of all stakeholders to plan, implement, and evaluate change. Moving from compliance to commitment for change can be assessed through tangible and intangible outcomes.

The change agent can use outcome measures to assess the process and results of change and to develop a deeper understanding of the needs of individuals, groups, and organizations. The complexity of change and the various pathways to achieve it require consideration of the multiple dimensions of change, including the needs of individuals and organizations to improve.

CASE STUDY

You have just accepted a new principalship after determining that you have the skills to move from a teaching position to an administrative one. You were successful at your previous school, and you are committed to work toward school improvement in a new setting. In researching this school prior to your employment, you realize that the current instructional and school improvement programs are ineffective.

You also realize that you will be responsible for bringing about improvement, and you can't do the job alone. The school has many challenges. It is on the state's academic "watch list" for not improving, and the student population is continuing to show declines in test scores. As the new instructional leader, what factors would you have to take into consideration to create an environment where change is encouraged? How would you manage the process as a change agent?

EXERCISES AND DISCUSSION QUESTIONS

1. Explain the *Change Framework* model and how it can be used to assess individual, group, and organizational needs. Suggest ways the framework overlaps to produce successful change. Reflect on how you would introduce yourself as a change-agent leader who is cognizant of all three of these needs when working with all stakeholders.
2. Determine how you will assess current change initiatives at your school and what is driving them to occur. Explain what federal mandates and state requirements have impacted the school at the local level.
3. Describe the components of a school improvement plan, and how these components should be created to bring about successful change. Analyze your own school improvement plan and explain how it was developed, implemented, and assessed.
4. List the components of the instructional program that need improvement and what resources may be needed to bring about change.
5. Explain how you would integrate the *Common Core State Standards* into the instructional program.
6. Describe the components of a *Whole Child Initiative* and how they can support school, faculty, and community improvement.
7. Research national, state, and local compliance initiatives that most schools are required to address and how you would explain them to faculty, resulting in tangible outcomes.
8. Reflect on ways to move from compliance to commitment for change and the impact this process will have on beliefs, values, and intangible outcomes.
9. Explain the value of a positive school culture on the change process and ways you, as the change agent, can go about creating it.
10. Describe ways to involve all stakeholders in making meaning of the need for change and the process to create it.

REFERENCES

Association of Supervisions and Curriculum Development. The whole child initiative. (n.d). Retrieved from www.ascd.org/whole-child.aspx?utm_source=ascd.org&utm_medium=web&utm_campaign=intelligent-search.

Common Core State Standards Initiative. (2012). Retrieved from www.corestandards.org.

Conner, D. (1993). *Managing at the speed of change.* New York: Villard Books.

DuFour, R. (2004). Schools as learning communities. *Educational Leadership, 61*(8), 6–11. Retrieved from www.plainfieldnjk12.org/pps_staff/docs/dufour_PLCs.pdf.

Duke, D. (2004). *The challenges of educational change.* New York: Pearson Education.

Evans, R. (1996). *The human side of school change.* San Francisco: Jossey-Bass.

Fullan, M. (1994). *Change forces.* London: Falmer.

Fullan, M. (2007). *The new meaning of educational change* (4th ed.). New York: Teachers College Press.

Gruenert, S. (2008). School culture, school climate: They are not the same thing. *Principal, 87*(4), 5–59. Retrieved from www.naesp.org/resources/2/Principal/2008/M-Ap56.pdf.

Illinois State Board of Education. (2010). School improvement monitoring prompt. Retrieved from www.isbe.net/sos/pdf/sip_monitoring.pdf.

Jorgensen, M., & Hoffman, J. (2003). *History of the No Child Left Behind Act (NCLB).* Retrieved from www.pearsonassessments.com/NR/rdonlyres/D8E33AAE-BED1-4743-98A1-BDF4D49D7274/0/HistoryofNCLB.pdf.

Kotter, J. (2002). *The heart of change.* Boston, MA: Harvard Business School Press.

Loukas, A. (2007). What is school climate? *Leadership Compass, 5*(1), 1–3. Retrieved from www.naesp.org/resources/2/Leadership_Compass/2007/LC2007v5n1a4.pdf.

National Commission on Excellence in Education. (1983). *A Nation at Risk.* Retrieved from www.scribd.com/doc/49151492/A-Nation-at-Risk.

School improvement plan template. (n.d.). Retrieved from www.michigan.gov/mde/0,1607,7-140-28753_38959---00.html.

Senge, P. (1999). *The dance of change.* New York: Doubleday.

Senge, P. (2006). *The fifth discipline.* New York: Doubleday.

Senge, P., Kleiner, A., Roberts, C., Ross, R., & Smith, B. (1994). *The fifth discipline field-book.* New York: Doubleday.

Stivers, J., & Cramer, S. (2009). *A teacher's guide to change.* Thousand Oaks, CA: Corwin.

Chapter Two

The School Leader as Change Agent

OBJECTIVES

At the conclusion of this chapter you will be able to:

1. Understand the role of the leader in developing, articulating, implementing, and stewarding a shared vision and mission by leading and managing change (ELCC 1.1, 1.2, 1.3, 1.4, 3.1, 3.2, ISLLC 1, 3).
2. Understand organizational structures, various roles and purposes of leadership, and ways to promote the success of students by leading all stakeholders in the change process (ELCC 1.4, 1.5, 2.1, 2.4, 3.1, 4.1, 4.2, 4.3, ISLLC 1, 2, 3, 4).
3. Understand leadership qualities, skills, and roles, and the importance of acting fairly with integrity to make decisions that establish a positive school climate in bringing about successful change (ELCC 2.1, 5.1, 5.2, 5.3, ISLLC 2, 5).
4. Understand ways and processes to engage and motivate faculty, staff, and community members to establish collaboration, communication, and organizational capacity to implement and sustain change for school improvement (ELCC 2.1, 2.2, 2.3, 2.4, 3.1, 3.2, 4.2, 6.1, 6.2, 6.3, ISLLC 1, 2, 4, 6).
5. Describe ways to build and sustain positive relationships with all stakeholders involved in the change process to promote shared leadership and responsibility for realizing the vision and mission of school improvement (ELCC 1.1, 1.2, 1.4, 1.5, 2.1, 2, 4, 3.1, 4.1, 4.2, 4.3, ISLLC 1, 3, 4, 5).

SCHOOL LEADERSHIP IN THE CHANGE PROCESS

Effective school leaders are educators who realize the need for school improvement and actively engage in initiating, implementing, and sustaining the change process. They are leaders because they demonstrate an understanding of the complexity of change as it impacts the three levels of the *Change Framework*: individual, organizational, and group needs (see figure 1.1.)

They strive to address these needs since they are able to identify how change will impact the school setting in a rapidly increasing results-driven climate. They are willing to take risks as they learn and execute the process of change. This is essential in developing a change process that effectively leads and engages others in achieving positive results.

Leaders continually reflect on the impact of their own skills within the context of change and monitor their own effectiveness during the change process. Organizations need to recognize change leaders since "the challenges of change encourage the development of a new kind of leader who understands that change is complex and brings about uncertainty—but is the cornerstone of growth and improvement" (Trybus, 2011, p. 35).

The change leader is invaluable to schools. Unfortunately, most schools may not realize or understand the importance of developing change leadership since this role is not clearly defined, and does not hold a formal title or job description. There is little if any training to be a change leader, and schools that are in the midst of change do not include a strategy to develop this form of leadership. Because of the vital role leadership plays in school improvement, developing change leaders should be integrated into the change process.

Even though there may be little or no formal recognition of change leaders' roles and responsibilities, they most likely exist in schools to varying degrees. It is a best practice, therefore, to carefully study and analyze how these leaders work in the school setting in order to define the factors that contribute to their success or failure. Gaining insight into the characteristics, qualities, and skills of change leaders is a necessary and a critical component to successful change.

What makes change leaders different from traditional school leaders? How can change leaders be developed so that the culture within the school is positively impacted, resulting in school improvement? What influence do change leaders have on motivating individuals to embrace change? How can change leaders be equipped to improve schools during the change process? What are the rewards of being a change-agent leader?

Figure 2.1. Change Leadership Development Model

One approach to addressing these questions is to strategically review the *Change Leadership Development Model* that can be applied to a school setting. Figure 2.1 illustrates the model that shows the components of identifying individuals, establishing roles, observing qualities, fostering skills, and offering rewards that are important considerations when developing change leaders.

Identifying Change Leaders

Schools in the midst of change need to have a broad base of leadership. The days of administrative leadership being responsible to make change happen is not adequate. Administrators, defined by their formal role and position, often begin the change process but cannot implement and sustain it without the collaboration and support of other school leaders. Identifying change leaders requires an examination of their role, function, and responsibilities since their need for engagement in the change process is often not clear.

Formal Leadership Positions

The complicated work of identifying the need and initiation of change is typically the responsibility of those in formal positions of authority beginning with school district leaders: superintendents, district office assistant superintendents, business managers, curriculum directors, and human resource directors. Leadership at the building level includes the principal, assistant principals, and in high schools department chairs.

The job responsibilities of these formal positions require staying attuned to know when change is essential and imminent due to accountability requirements in policy, mandates, and district and school improvement needs. Reviewing district organizational charts can clearly define which employee serves the organization in a specific position so that the management of change is shared and efficiently executed.

This process creates a *division of labor* when change is complex, and also indicates the specialist in the area most impacted by change who would logically take the dominant leadership role. For example, in the case of *second-order change,* which involves restructuring schools, the entire administrative team would be involved, with the superintendent and board of education making major decisions.

When reassigning faculty teaching positions, the building principal, working closely with the human resource director, may take more of the lead role. Major changes in curriculum, instruction, and assessment would be under the auspices of the director of curriculum and instruction. The business manager most likely would be involved in all change initiatives, due to the need to analyze costs.

The *division of labor* is essential since the authority to make decisions and direct the work of others takes expertise. Yet the need to work as a unit of administration in these formal leadership positions is a necessary requirement to effectively help all employees work toward successful change. This in essence is a collaborative process and often achieves a synergistic outcome.

The role of the district office should be one of support and assistance to the school leaders who are responsible for instructional improvement and student learning. The structure of the district office should be able to facilitate the building level needs, so that leadership at the district level can assist with project management, fiscal accountability, and indicators of student learning outcomes (Hanover Research, 2011).

Your school district organizational chart defines the framework of authority and shows the relationship of management to all functions of the schools, the supervision of personnel, and the *chain of command.* The size of the school district often determines the structure and the number of formal leaders which is also dependent on fiscal resources to pay for administrative salaries.

A bureaucratic structure is most common due to the complexity of managing schools and the necessity to define the chain of command. This will provide clarity and differentiation of roles and status for all stakeholders.

Moreover it services as a cost-effective approach to change that ultimately values and supports resource management.

The concept of a *bureaucracy* is credited to Max Weber, a German sociologist who in the early 1900s did a comparative study of many organizations to determine the most efficient and scientific way to operate (Owens & Valesky, 2007). The traditional view of an organization known as a "bureaucracy" is also more commonly called the *"factory model."*

Weber's theory had six characteristics that still exist in many schools today. These include: management by rules, division of labor, formal hierarchical structure, personnel hired on grounds of technical competence, managers as salaried officials, and written documents (of decisions, rules, and actions taken by the organization) that are formulated and recorded in writing (Cutajar, 2010).

Since school district bureaucracies have been modeled after large-scale organizations for decades, the challenge to make them work in the twenty-first century with the recognized need for shared leadership roles to address change has been difficult. The term *bureaucracy* often has negative connotations since it portrays a top-down management structure. Weber's bureaucratic theory contributed to the creation of organizational charts. Figure 2.2 is an example of a typical school organizational chart that has the characteristics of a bureaucratic structure.

Visually a bureaucratic organizational structure looks very rigid, where all decisions start at the top of the chart, typically at the superintendent and/or the building principal level. One caution for formal leaders is to realize that delegation of the work of change to those on the bottom can be met with resistance. *Top-down decision making* related to change is difficult for teachers to accept, which is why formal leaders in bureaucratic school organizations need to be mindful of the rigidity that it implies.

Selectively knowing when top-down decision making is appropriate due to the nature and need for efficiency is, however, very important. For example, top-down decisions are made when the demand for quick and rapid responses to issues dealing with safety, school stability, and situations where alternative solutions are not possible is warranted.

The fast-paced environment of rapidly changing circumstances may require administrative decisions to be made with relatively little input from others. Another perspective that the change leader has to consider is when to engage stakeholders in decision making so that the organization is vested to act on the decisions. The value of collaboration to problem solve is the mark of a quality leader who is mindful of going beyond the title of the position

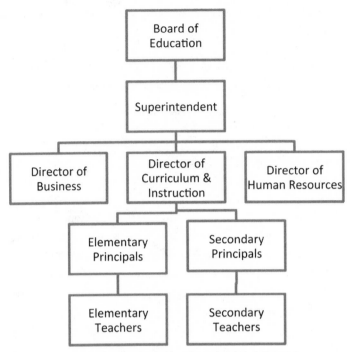

Figure 2.2.   Typical School District Organizational Structure

and individual decision making so that a *professional learning community* is formed and can function within a bureaucratic school structure.

Formal change leaders need to examine the responsibility they have in creating a *shared vision* for change. A shared vision requires understanding the existing school conditions that require change, and leading others in a climate of trust and mutual respect. A shared vision requires long-term planning to determine where the organization is and where it needs to be in the process of change; therefore all stakeholders should be welcomed to voice their concerns and share suggestions for improvement.

A shared vision is needed to avoid conflict when the school system is disrupted, requiring individuals to leave their comfort zone and change practices for the sake of the organization. Consequently the leader needs to understand how to facilitate groups to envision what a quality school looks like and define the characteristics that the school strives to develop in the process of change.

The school principal, in the role of *change leader* and catalyst for change at the building level, must realize that a shared vision is critical for school improvement. The principal needs to be a visionary who uses his or her formal leadership position strategically. Being knowledgeable, thoughtful, insightful, and reflective takes skill development not only to create the vision, but to lead others to implement and actualize the shared vision.

There is a tremendous amount of pressure on the school principal to bring about change due to the existence and expansion of school improvement plans each year. Of all the formal positions that make up the administrative team, the principal is the most highly charged to solve the problem of the achievement gap among diverse groups of students, and to lead standards-based reforms that impact teaching and learning. The principal is accountable to provide measurable results as part of his or her performance review.

The constant turbulence this creates requires leaders to accept and realize they cannot do the job alone, yet cannot appear to delegate and leave the job to others. Even with direct control and responsibility of the school and its programs, the insightful principal constantly reviews the school structure, successful and unsuccessful instructional practices, and begins to identify the *informal leaders* who are instrumental in making positive change happen.

Informal Leadership Roles

The collective sense of purpose inherent in a *shared vision* of change requires the recognition of school leaders who may not have formal positions of leadership yet exude a tremendous amount of influence on the school culture. These *informal leaders* have strengths, skills, and talents that emerge through personal attributes that are seen by others. Formal leaders in an organization can influence informal leaders by recognizing that they exist, and work to capitalize and utilize them in ways that are rewarding for both the school and the individual.

This type of recognition utilizes a model of *loose coupling* which impacted education in the early 1970s as school bureaucracies struggled to meet increasing demands while remaining isolated in change efforts. This view suggests that

> "the technical core" of education—detailed decisions about what should be taught at any given time, how it should be taught, what students should be expected to learn at any given time, how they should be grouped within classrooms for purposes of instruction, what they should be required to do to demonstrate their knowledge, and, perhaps most importantly, how their learning

should be evaluated—resides in individual classrooms, not in the organizations that surround them. (Elmore, 2000, p. 5–6)

The degree to which schools acknowledge loose coupling directly relates to the extent to which informal leaders are nurtured within the school culture. Some schools are hard pressed to find informal leaders, which may be due to the fact that they are so tightly controlled by formal leaders, therefore giving little opportunity for informal leaders to emerge.

Creating conditions and opportunities for informal leadership to develop is critical in the change process. If there are rare moments for engagement of informal leaders, then the impetus for change and the *shared meaning* of change is thwarted. Lack of informal leadership discourages those for whom change means loss rather than growth, risk rather than innovation, and uncertainty rather than motivation to make change happen for the good of the organization.

Identifying the *informal change-agent leader* can be fairly straightforward. A place to start might be looking at school structures beyond the organizational chart that identify and require informal leaders to serve in additional roles beyond their contractual obligations. These might include union, teacher, and parental leaders, who are either voted for or appointed by constituents to represent groups within the school organization. Being recognized by one's peers is a sure sign that these individuals are the right informal leaders to add to the formal leadership team responsible for change.

Teacher union presidents are critical leaders in supporting or preventing school change. With their endorsement and power they can help turn ideas into implemented programs that cannot be accomplished through formal leadership alone (Johnson, 2010). Successful school principals discuss change initiatives with teacher union presidents and ask for assistance in identifying who among the teachers would be qualified, interested, and willing to serve on change teams.

This relationship-building approach might be the future of strong union administration partnerships, but hard to achieve. "Every local union elects a president who is well positioned to influence teachers and schooling by shaping local priorities, building coalitions to achieve shared purposes, negotiating the contract, and working either collaboratively or contentiously with school officials" (Johnson et al., 2009, p. 375).

While recognizing that competing interests and obligations exist, both union and formal leaders must be willing to bring differences into honest and open discussion. Without this type of dialogue, there may not be an opportunity for the proposed practices to develop into meaningful change. The result of this change will not benefit the organization, individuals, and most importantly the students in the school.

Informal leadership must include the *teacher leader*. The movement toward teacher leadership involves a shift from top-down hierarchical leadership structures and a move toward teamwork, shared decision making, and community building (Wynne, 2001). *Teacher leadership* can take many forms through assigned nonsupervisory positions such as department chair, grade-level team leader, faculty mentor, curriculum specialist, literacy coach, or lead content teacher.

Teacher leaders may also serve on textbook committees, curricular councils, staff development teams, strategic planning groups, technology teams, and school improvement committees. Sometimes, teacher leaders emerge by nature of their experience, disposition, and relationships with others who admire, trust, and support the teacher leader in any initiative that is deemed of importance.

The practice of teacher leadership according to Katzenmeyer (as cited in Raffanti, 2008) can be stated as: "teachers who lead within and beyond the classroom, identify with and contribute to a community of teacher learners and leaders, and influence others towards improved educational practice" (p. 58). This statement reinforces the principles of shared responsibility, empowerment, and collaboration to leading school change.

Because teacher leaders are powerful influences on formal leaders and other colleagues, they are critical in shaping the *school culture*. When the school culture is stabilized and focused on change it is most likely the result of teacher leaders who support others by interacting with formal leaders and engage in peer leadership. They operate on multiple levels using their experience, skills, and collaborative approaches to unite the bureaucratic hierarchical school structure with the informal leadership that may be emerging.

Forging these relationships brings *top-down* and *bottom-up decision making* together which is a strategic component of a quality school facing change. Compare the teacher who feels afraid to ask questions about change since it is imposed from the top to the teacher who has a proven ability to change and be adaptable and is encouraged by formal leaders to offer constructive questions, ideas and creative problem-solving approaches. When the environment supports innovative thinking rather than command-and-control management, the end product of change is innovative and psychologically more acceptable and engaging.

Teacher leaders understand the need for their involvement in *shared decision making* and approach the division of labor in a bureaucratic organization as more of a challenge than an impediment. Over time, however, relationships can lead to successful change outcomes. As teacher leaders model a sense of ownership in the shared vision of change, the traditional bureaucratic management approach becomes obviously no longer effective and a new paradigm emerges that is more aligned with the individual, group, and organizational needs for change.

Even with a compelling shared vision for school improvement, teacher leaders cannot exist without the support of the building principal. Commitment alone is not enough to establish a learning community that values teacher leaders as an essential human resource.

The principal can sustain and develop teacher leaders by realizing that opportunities for teachers to meet and study issues need to occur. The principal also needs to be sensitive to the impact of teacher leadership on peer relationships, and willingly provide resources through training, release time, and even financial stipends. These steps are imperative to develop enduring relationships between formal leaders and teacher leaders.

The movement toward teacher leadership for twenty-first-century schools is so strong that in 2008 *teacher leader standards* were established. These help address the question: Can all teachers be teacher leaders? The standards establish a framework to support the identification and development of teacher leaders by state departments of education.

Many states have created teacher leader endorsements, universities and colleges are developing teacher leader programs of study, and school districts eagerly seek to nurture and grow teacher leadership. The following domains express the roles and skills needed to be a teacher leader:

Domain I: Fostering a Collaborative Culture to Support Educator Development and Student Learning
Domain II: Accessing and Using Research to Improve Practice and Student Learning
Domain III: Promoting Professional Learning for Continuous Improvement
Domain IV: Facilitating Improvements in Instruction and Student Learning
Domain V: Promoting the Use of Assessments and Data for School and District Improvement

Domain VI: Improving Outreach and Collaboration with Families and
Community
Domain VII: Advocating for Student Learning and the Profession

(Teacher Leadership Exploratory Consortium, 2012, p. 9)

Developing informal roles to support change leadership is one step toward building capacity within an organization to move forward and embrace change. Realizing people's competence to be engaged in *participatory management* is another approach that goes beyond a top-down bureaucratic structure and motivates stakeholders to play a welcome role in the change process. There are many benefits of participatory management when tough decisions for the distribution of resources, assignment changes, program development, and change management stress the organization and formal leaders.

By increasing the involvement of others, there is more likelihood of discovering multiple approaches to problem solving and strategic empowerment of shared ownership of the problem. Without disclosure of the problems facing the organization and without providing an avenue for others to address the problems, the burden of success and the doom of failure is the ultimate responsibility of top management. This approach does little to motivate those in informal roles who aspire to formal leadership positions, since the risk of failure is a high price to pay for career advancement.

Rather, participatory management through shared decision making and empowerment can begin to establish a learning organization that inspires and motivates new leaders to accept more responsibility and attain greater job satisfaction. It offers a model to build future leaders by giving them a chance to engage in making good decisions as part of a team of formal and informal leaders who have the skills to facilitate groups, brainstorm ideas, reach compromise, and commit to the execution of change plans.

Assigned versus Voluntary Tasks

School experiences either as a learner, teacher, or administrator often include the assignment or appointment to serve on a committee or a particular team. Some people might experience feelings of joy in being chosen because they value the public acknowledgment of their ability to contribute to a particular task.

Also, it may not be clear as to how or why someone is chosen, but feelings of worth in being one of a chosen few often exist. Conversely, feelings might be completely different because some individuals may feel anxious or even afraid since they are completely unaware of what is expected, do not like being singled out in front of others, and lack the confidence to do the job.

Individual responses to task assignments are unpredictable to the change leader. What might be thought of as an opportunity given to a willing worker to play an informal leadership role may be misconstrued as an imposition (i.e., role incongruity). The change leader may not see the assigned task as a burden to the individual, nor have any motives to take advantage of anyone. The assigned individual, however, may see the appointment differently. This could be due to a conflicting issue that accompanies assignment for extra duties beyond the workday.

Without mention of contractual obligations for additional pay in the form of an hourly rate that is often part of the teachers' negotiated contract, or a stipend that could be monetary or a reduced teaching load, the fear turns to resistance. Without clear communication as to the implications of this assigned task, the reluctant individual seeks clarity before committing to the task, and the change-agent leader has to anticipate what approach will alleviate these issues if he or she values the assigned person's expertise and involvement.

On the same committee, however, other members may see the assigned task as a way to present themselves as a future leader. They welcome the opportunity since they have confidence in their ability to contribute to the task, and in the process grow in service and stature within the organization. In this case, the change leader feels encouraged in making the right appointment, but nevertheless should closely monitor this enthusiastic committee member who may or may not be recognized as an informal leader by other members of the committee.

The strategic change leader thinks carefully about the diversity of the membership when formulating committees, task forces, and special assignment groups. Besides individual needs, establishing diverse perspectives to problem solve an issue reflects the growing demands for a multicultural approach.

Knowing the history of the organization and the committee structures of the past may indicate the need for a more inclusive approach that will help connect people of different ages, gender, and racial groups. Inviting participation to be responsive to multicultural communication does take commitment on the part of the change leader, but over time the culture of the organization should embrace these opportunities as opposed to rejecting them.

Another approach to consider is asking for *leader volunteers* for a particular task. This might be an appropriate approach for those tasks that are not as high stakes and may be short term. For example, asking for volunteers to attend an event such as an open house, parent night, or college recruitment event may be appropriate since these events do not involve a prolonged amount of time or commitment.

Volunteering to organize a social event, a retirement tea, or a school dance is also feasible. The volunteer can be identified for his or her willingness to serve and acknowledged by a simple thank-you note or a free lunch which reinforces a good deed. Committee volunteerism is also an interesting approach when the change leader isn't sure who is best qualified, has available time, or is willing to serve.

Opportunities to be part of a task force or a project management team encourages talented people to grow within the school. This helps identify the person who may get overlooked in some cases because the person is non-tenured faculty, new to the school district, or simply unassuming. The volunteers are often enthusiastic, motivated, and eager to get engaged. By offering them an opportunity to serve, they feel reaffirmed in being part of the school community.

Some of the hazards for consideration in building change leaders are that similarity in thought, position, experience, and knowledge might speed up decision making but does not lead to innovative change and new ideas. Encouraging debate, challenging assumptions, and valuing diversity help organizations become adaptable in pioneering change efforts that may seem unconventional but will become exciting growth opportunities (Hamel, 2012).

Formal and informal change leaders who represent various departments within the school must combine efforts to blend diversity of thought, age, experience, knowledge, gender, and culture in order to meet the growing needs of school change and improvement.

CHANGE LEADERSHIP DEVELOPMENT

Educational leaders promote the success of all students guided by the vision of learning that is supported through the school culture. Since school change is so complex, it requires a framework for leadership that isn't defined solely by hierarchy within the organization, but rather by the ability to motivate others to also perform leadership roles. No one leader can accomplish change without utilizing the talents and skills of others. As schools improve, so must leaders improve by realizing the multiple influential roles required to enable others to commit to change.

The challenging tasks of school change need to be clearly communicated, fostered, and shared so that synergism drives shared leadership within the organization. Within a school setting synergy recognizes that a cohesive team of leaders can collectively manage change far more effectively than one leader alone.

LEADERSHIP ROLES AND MODELS

Several models of leadership can effectively guide change-agent roles in leading the change process. The *shared leadership model* relies on formal leaders getting the work done through participatory decision making, assignment of tasks to others, and group work. A balance between relationship building and task development is critical so that the work and pace of change is effectively managed. The leader of this model performs the roles of *collaborator, facilitator*, and *decision maker* within the group so that leadership is shared. Therefore responsibility is shared also (Green, 2013).

As a result of school improvement needs, *distributed leadership*—a form of shared leadership—has also emerged through various levels of a school community. *Distributed leadership* acts on the achievement of goals through purposeful assignment of tasks, which is crucial in the change process. The tasks may be specific to grade levels, curriculum projects, or community initiatives.

With many school improvement requirements, a distributed leadership model shifts the participation from a few individuals to many who have specific expertise that is needed to guide the undertaking. This model generates opportunities for group interaction and *team building*, which grows both formal and informal teacher leaders and establishes collegiality with a purpose.

Another model applicable to the change process is the *situational leadership model*. Since there is no one way to lead especially during times of change, leaders will find it necessary to adapt their style. A situational change leader uses telling, selling, participating, and delegating styles to work with others

(Hersey, Blanchard, & Johnson, 2001). These leadership styles are purposely altered depending on the maturity level of the followers and their need to be directed to complete a task versus relationship orientation.

In this model the leader's role may be that of *coach* giving specific directions and close supervision, versus support where there is more delegation and freedom for others to engage in making decisions (Green, 2013). The situational leadership approach varies and may be hard to utilize without some leadership experience and knowledge of the individuals involved. The change leader has to use good judgment in knowing what style is most appropriate for the situation and task.

The model does suggest a flexible and versatile leadership style that may appeal to a variety of stakeholders with different preferences and needs for engagement depending on the situation, people being led, and the leader's own preferred style. It is important to realize that what may work in one situation may not work in another which is true of both first- *and second-order change* experiences. The situational leader is well suited to be a change agent since adaptive skills are necessary to deal with the complexity of change.

Fullan (2001) states, "Energetic-enthusiastic-hopeful leaders 'cause' greater moral purpose in themselves, bury themselves in change, naturally build relationships and knowledge, and seek coherence to consolidate moral purpose" (p. 7). Moral purpose is not only a leadership quality but an essential component of a quality school facing change. *Moral leadership* is built from widely shared values and beliefs that motivate people to act not for self-interest, but rather because it is the right thing to do for the school.

Building on the concept of moral leadership, Sergiovanni (1992) suggests that the relationship between the leader and led is based on a covenant that is a "shared and a fundamental agreement that all members of a community subscribe to and mutually reinforce" (Sergiovanni in Evans, 1996, p. 175). The application of the moral leadership model to school change is logical in that the covenant helps *make meaning* of the change and defines the need for change that is universally understood.

The leader's role is that of visionary and steward of change. The holistic approach of moral leadership complements a *shared leadership model* and the foundation for developing change that depends on whole school engagement and transformation.

Transformational leadership also relies on building a followership that values and wants change for both personal and organizational improvement. Transformational leaders know how to utilize their role to help people transform their thinking about teaching and learning so that the school community benefits (Evans, 1996). By investing in the people, all stakeholders are involved in transforming the organization. There is a commitment and a bond that is inspired by the transformational leader who realizes the vision of improvement and change must be one that is shared.

Since an inherent difficulty in transforming schools exists, the role of the transformational leader is one of advocating change in ways that makes sense to others. Transformational change leaders highly value expanded roles of followers so that their needs for growth during the period of change are considered. As a change agent, the transformational leader is very influential and highly motivational since actions are purposefully crafted to help followers psychologically, morally, and intellectually accept the vision and need for change.

When schools go through major restructuring as second-order change, transformational leadership provides a departure from what exists and isn't working to what is needed to survive and improve. For example, large urban high schools struggle to deal with academic, social, and behavior issues that stem from the lack of personalization and individualization to help students succeed (Trybus, 2001).

This concept can be reinforced by the following statement: "The reform effort to redesign schools calls upon strategic action intended to help school leaders make choices as to how they will restructure the educational system. This poses challenges, as the leaders have to 'let go' of old ways in favor of systemic reform" (Trybus, 2001, p. 17). This requires a sense of confidence and competence by school-change leaders.

Many cases of transforming large high schools to smaller academies require both *transformation leadership* and *moral leadership* to help struggling students who are at risk of dropping out of school. High school reform is just one example where change leaders have to assess their role and be adaptable since transforming an existing system that has been in existence for decades is a major undertaking. The eclectic nature of leadership roles and styles is needed since the complexity of leading change in various diverse and complex school systems will not be successful with just one approach.

Lastly, according to Greenleaf (2002), the model of *servant leadership* condemns leadership as power and control, and states:

A new moral principle is emerging which holds that the only authority deserving one's allegiance is that which is freely and knowingly granted by the led to the leaders in response to, and in perception to, the clearly evident servant nature of the leader. (p. 10)

Leadership depends on the trust individuals have for one another in any role, formal or informal. The *servant leader* is trusted because the top priority is investment in people whom the leader cares for and nurtures. This is a critical role for the change-agent leader since serving others means understanding the human condition and the anxiety that change can create. The servant leader guides and shows the way to embark on the change journey through inspiring others while eliciting their confidence, competence, and pursuit of common goals.

In change situations the role of servant leader reaffirms an ethical approach to let go of what exists and lead others into unknown territory, not for any personal gain or influence of grandiose ideas. Rather, the servant change agent uses less positional power and control and is successful by showing empathy to others, listening intently to concerns, and acting with honesty and justice for the good of the organization.

The roles of change leaders can be defined through the examination of various leadership models: *shared, distributed, situational, moral, transformational, and servant.* Each leadership model has some similar and some unique components. What makes them suitable to apply to the change process is the focus on the relationship between leader and follower and the unpretentious nature of leadership which is reliant on a different form of power than is typical in a hierarchical organizational structure.

Power is associated with leadership in that it influences others to take action to change. Leadership actions can be inviting or persuasive and demanding. Formal and informal leaders exercise power in many ways that are traditionally described in relationship to the source of power. These sources of power were defined by French and Raven in 1959 (in Northouse, 2010) as:

Legitimate power. Associated with having status or formal job authority.
Reward power. Derived from having the capacity to provide rewards to others.
Coercive power. Derived from having the capacity to penalize or punish others.
Expert power. Based on followers' perceptions of the leader's competence.
Referent power. Based on followers' identification and liking for the leader.

(Northouse, 2010, p. 7)

The change leader will have to draw on multiple *sources of power* in response to the change drivers (figure 1.2). When dealing with mandates and policy decisions, position power that is legitimate and perhaps even linked to rewards and coercion is most likely evident in change scenarios. Even though formal leaders have power available to them by virtue of their job status, extreme use of legitimate power can result in negative consequences and resistance.

An example of this is mandatory curricular changes that require teachers to abandon certain classroom practices as a result of a top-down decision (sometimes from the district office) to implement a new computer-based program. This change may be due to federal and state requirements.

However, rather than engaging teachers and developing a change strategy, leaders use their power and often overlook the needed personal approach. The pressure and the timeliness to bring about this instructional change frequently drive the formal leader to evoke legitimate power and reward those employees that comply, and penalize those that do not.

When leaders recognize the influence of their personal power, they may use a softer, more humanistic approach. *Referent* and *expert* power can be effective when the leader is acknowledged by others as having expertise and is likable. Power is earned through relationship building that can be enhanced by using change tools (see chapter 3).

For example, in the scenario requiring a curricular change perhaps in reading skills, the leader is knowledgeable about literacy but is also conscious of the need to facilitate a group that will collectively reach a shared decision about what particular curricular changes should be made and how they will be made. This approach uses power in a way that does not elevate fear or resistance to change.

Leadership Qualities and Skills

Much has been written about leadership qualities and characteristics, and in relationship to being a change-agent leader they cannot be overlooked. Since the process of change is so dynamic, leading school change requires personal and professional qualities that are above reproach. Since the core of leadership is effectiveness it is important to examine the question of what qualities and characteristics are required of the change-agent leader in order to maximize successful change.

There is a legitimate point of view that emerges during the change process, and stakeholders might wonder what is in it for the leader? The correlation between personal gains and school gains is a realistic expectation that can be acceptable if the leader is seen as credible. In other words, if the school shows improvement as a result of change should the leader gain credibility? If the school becomes dysfunctional as a result of change, does the leader lose credibility? A change-agent leader has to have *credibility* that stems from the perception of the followers in order to be successful. Covey (1991) suggests

> perception and credibility problems may ultimately result in complicated knots, what we often call "personality conflict" or "communication break-down." Credibility problems are far more difficult to resolve, primarily because each of the people involved thinks he sees the world as it is rather than as he is. (p. 109)

When a change-agent leader thinks and acts with a sense of "I'm right" when others think and do not act because they disagree, tension will occur within the organization and most certainly impact the school culture. Ways to address this scenario depend on the ability for the change-agent leader to be an *effective communicator* who can also display humility.

Communication lines are instrumental in explaining and demonstrating positive and forthright attitudes and behaviors regarding the process of change. If the change-agent leader can communicate the what, why, and how of change in a sincere and realistic manner there is more likelihood of gaining credibility and being seen as *trustworthy*.

Leaders have to be transparent in explaining the need for change so that followers can become engaged in addressing it in a shared leadership approach. *Transparency* means being forthright and sincere in communicating with others the need for first- or second-order change and then inviting input through a defined role for every member engaged in the change process.

To make progress during times of change, leaders must demonstrate several important components of communication including clarity, talking points, addressing questions, and continual timely updates. *Resistance to change* often occurs because stakeholders are unclear about the purpose, direction, and approach in implementing the change. Skepticism develops, which leads to fear simply because the change-agent leader is unclear in communicating with others.

A simple approach is to develop talking points that repeatedly provide consistent communication so that what is said to one group is the same as what is said to another. This also helps address rumors and inappropriate accusations that derail change. Follow-up meetings that address emerging questions will also provide a forum for continued updates so that resisters can become informed and eventually evolve into supporters.

Since the change agent is the point person in leading and facilitating the change process, he or she must possess *inspirational* characteristics that project a positive communication style. This is derived from perceptions of the change agents' attitude which can be seen as positive, inviting, and invigorating. Inspirational change leaders have four unexpected qualities. According to Goffee and Jones (2000) these include selectively showing their weaknesses which reveals they are approachable; relying on intuition to gauge the appropriate time and course of their actions; managing others with empathy; and revealing differences to capitalize on their uniqueness.

The inspirational change agent is one who is admired because he or she exhibits resilience in the face of change, and encourages others to have faith that change is possible. *Resiliency* during times of change portrays the change agent as an optimistic believer that the organization and the people in it can overcome challenges and not only survive but thrive as a result of moving from what is not working to what holds promise to achieve better outcomes.

People like to affiliate themselves with an inspirational leader who is resilient. Stakeholders are more willing to become followers, even if they have some skepticism in the message. Inspirational change leaders are very visionary and do an exceptional job in communicating the vision every chance they have in working with groups within the school community.

They also believe in the power of individual conversations that provide the opportunity to build support and credibility. They invest in the time it takes to move people to believe in change since they realize relationships, along with leadership qualities and skills, maximize *individual and collective efficacy* that change will happen.

Bandura (1997) in his theory of self-efficacy explains that "people's beliefs in their capabilities to produce desired effects by their actions" (preface) are very relevant to change processes since the impact of the inspirational change leader is only thwarted by an individual's lack of ability to be efficacious. This means that if individuals feel they cannot change, they most likely will not. "Perceived self-efficacy is concerned not with the number of skills you have, but with what you believe you can do with what you have under a variety of circumstances" (p. 37).

Obviously change does present a variety of circumstances in which individuals and change leaders have to not only rely on the inner personal efficacy factors, but also the collective efficacy of an organization. When individual and groups feel change is possible and needed, it is more likely to occur and be successfully implemented.

The interdependence of individuals working together is a very powerful factor on the influence that groups who coordinate change strategies have on each other. "Belief of collective efficacy affects the sense of mission and purpose of a system, the strength of common commitment to what it seeks to achieve, how well its members work together to produce results, and the group's resiliency in the face of difficulties" (Bandura, 1997, p. 469).

No matter the extent to which change leaders are trustworthy, credible, transparent, and inspirational, they are also responsible and *accountable* for results. The external measure of change requires change leaders to accept their role for results and demonstrate understanding in learning how to be accountable. In the face of this tremendous challenge, accountability must be an *ongoing learned skill* which the change leader continuously works toward. This skill is developed by learning how to collect, analyze, and act on existing data, as well as learning how to create surveys and instruments which may not exist in the school setting (see chapter 4).

Besides national and state forms of data, classroom teachers often rely on and need evidence of effective classroom results in order to believe that change is working at the closest level of impact, which most often is with the students. *Research-based* decision making should be a common practice that supports change, fosters innovation, and continuous improvement. The change leader is an *ongoing learner* since change is a dynamic enterprise and requires constant adaptability and reframing in order to produce the desired results.

Effective change leaders combine personal qualities with tangible results so that they not only have credibility due to what they say they are going to accomplish but results that show they have actually achieved those accomplishments. Even though they are accountable, change leaders cannot bring about these results alone. They are more likely to be successful through the formation of change teams.

Realizing goals through actions and by working with teams, measurable results are more favorable and build confidence and credibility in the leader.

It is not only a matter of sharing the vision for change but demonstrating the knowledge and skills that are realized in working with others. This leads to tangible data which all stakeholders value in the process of change, and which is needed to change beliefs of those followers who are in doubt of the change process.

Change Leadership Rewards

With the realization of the challenges, turmoil, and the various roles change leaders acknowledge and accept, what then is the motivation to be a change leader? Assessing whether one possesses the qualities and the skills for change leadership, what factors should be considered in becoming a change-agent leader in schools? What are the rewards?

Just as there are a variety of leadership qualities and skills that are needed for school change, there are different ways to find rewards in change agentry depending on the individual needs of the formal or informal leader. A certain amount of *interpersonal intelligence* is needed to determine what motivates people to do the work of change, and *intrapersonal intelligence* to turn inward and reflect on one's actions and behaviors to find change work personally rewarding (Goleman, 1995). Interpersonal rewards come from success of working with others due to the ability to understand and work cooperatively and collaboratively on change initiatives.

Change is socially engaging and when the work is done in conjunction with others, feelings of pride in developing a sense of community are gratifying. *Intrinsic motivation* through intangible rewards includes feelings of enthusiasm and confidence that are found through the work of leading successful change. Of course being recognized and appreciated is motivational; however, obtaining feedback from others may not occur and should not deter developing as a change leader. Even with persistent setbacks, the change leader finds the quest of mastering change invigorating and therefore an opportunity to overcome personal and institutional obstacles.

Extrinsic motivation may come in the form of job advancement as a result of successful change leadership. Extrinsic rewards in moving up the *career ladder* may lead to informal leaders becoming formally recognized and appointed to school administration. This can lead to supervision of faculty and staff, but perhaps more importantly lead to school leadership that is change savvy. For example, the teacher leader who develops referent power may find he or she wants and is willing to accept positional power in order to more effectively and deliberately bring about change for school improvement.

The intrinsic and extrinsic rewards of change leadership parallel *Herzberg's two-factor theory of motivation* (in Owens & Valesky, 2007). In this theory, motivation is not seen as a single dimension but rather is composed of two separate, independent factors:

1. *Motivational factors*, which lead to job satisfaction.
2. *Maintenance factors*, which must be sufficiently present in order for motivational factors to come into play and when not sufficiently present can block motivation and can lead to job dissatisfaction (p. 389).

In other words, many conditions within the school environment impact motivation (*satisfiers*) and can lead to job satisfaction. In promoting change leaders, "achievement, recognition, the challenge of the work itself, responsibility, advancement and promotion, and personal or professional growth" are potential rewards that can become motivational factors (Owens & Valesky, 2007, p. 390).

Maintenance factors (also called *hygiene factors*) such as salary, working conditions, job security, and attitudes and policies of administration in themselves may not be motivational. However, according to Herzberg's theory, they may reduce dissatisfaction and create conditions that more favorably allow motivation to occur. This concept is essential in preventing employee attrition from dissatisfaction.

When maintenance factors such as low salaries, unpleasant work conditions, dysfunctional technology, and poor relationships with others are not properly addressed they will become *dissatisfiers* and can impact the performance of the change leader. Both motivational and maintenance factors have to be considered realistically in order to realize the rewards of change leadership in school settings.

Lastly the rewards of being part of *school improvement* efforts can spur the change agent to advance from team member to team leader. Being part of *capacity building* to support change for improvement means preparing the organization to accept challenges and opportunities in proactive ways. While some may be frustrated with school improvement plans and initiatives that are slow in realizing successful outcomes, the organization needs leadership to build capacity and renew efforts to develop collective responsibility for change.

This may take the form of facilitating professional development, developing a critical mass of informal leaders to become future formal leaders, and providing or redirecting resources that may not have been allocated to school improvement. Fullan (2007) suggests *"leveraging leadership"* which provides direction to the organization and is at the heart of sustainability. When leaders find others who are successful at school improvement and who are receiving intrinsic and extrinsic rewards, the next generation of change leaders evolves and builds capacity for change throughout the organization.

BUILDING THE CHANGE TEAM

Creating collective efficacy within schools to achieve change requires a plan to develop a *change team*. According to Bandura (1997):

> The effective exercise of collective action involves more complex, socially mediated paths of influence than does individual self-direction. People have to depend upon one another in performing tasks and in carrying out their complementary roles. Group success requires effective interdependent linkage of tasks, skills, and roles. Group members not only have to coordinate what they are doing individually with the work of others, but they are affected by the beliefs, motivation, and quality of performance of their co-workers. (p. 468)

The change team is a special action force that can help accelerate change and create "buy-in" within the organization.

For this reason, members have to be chosen from the major constituencies within the school. A cross section of administrators, teachers, parents, board members, union representatives, community members, and in some cases students can be identified as change team members depending on the size and scope of the change initiative.

Strategically identifying the membership is key since the role of the change team is to provide input into the planning, implementation, and sustainability of the change. The insight of this team is needed to establish a *shared vision* that leads to coordination and development of the action plan. The interdependent roles of change team members can be clearly seen in figure 2.3 which illustrates some of the skills to be considered for successful change team development.

Figure 2.3. Building the Change Team

This group of individuals, when working collectively, can steer the change as it unfolds and function as a shared leadership group together with the change leader. As the change project expands and interfaces with individuals and other groups in the school system, the change team must be equipped to face challenges and offer solutions. With this role, the change team members must represent both formal and informal authority.

People in positions of power working with informal leaders model openness to ideas, sharing of diverse experiences, and *reaching consensus* on important decisions. This will help the process of change to address school improvement, as it impacts the school culture and builds organizational capacity for innovation and creative problem solving.

Change team members also need to be knowledgeable and exhibit project credibility so that they are seen as experts on the topic. When possible, internal school members should fulfill this role, but outside experts may also need to serve on the team, or at least be available for consultation. Identifying levels of expertise on the topics requiring change is critical to success.

When people are recognized for their level of knowledge and expertise in a particular topic, they are more willing to take an active role in the change. Not only do they have expertise, but they most likely know how to access outside resources including research-based practices and exemplary programs that have proven results.

Even with a vested interest in the proposed change, teams need members who have the dispositions to be mediators who seek to reach consensus. The mediator is a good listener who knows how to communicate honestly to resolve team conflicts. Team conflicts can stem from disagreements that can cause gridlock in the change process if not properly addressed.

The team mediator listens to varying points of view without taking (or giving) offense and facilitates working toward consensus. Rather than letting a dominant member determine the ebb and flow of decisions, the mediator realizes people need to take ownership for their own actions, and feel that their voice is heard even when questioned.

Disagreements can lead to debate, encouraging investigation to gather more information. For example, team members may have technical skills in a particular problem and rely on their experience to determine their point of view. Even with this background, though, experience, researching and gathering the ideas of others may be a healthier approach for the change team to explore before accepting or rejecting a recommendation (see chapter 3).

Teamwork can raise the quality of the decision and hopefully lower the risk of failure. Members of the team must be committed to work collaboratively and recognize and support one another. The benefits of teamwork to the school are evident when the outcome of the change initiative is successful, and the team (not any one individual) is recognized for being effective.

SUMMARY

The process of change requires effective leaders who understand the needs of the organization, individuals, and groups that are focused on improving schools. Change leaders can be identified based on formal and informal leadership positions. Formal leadership positions are needed at both the district and school level to efficiently and effectively manage change. Organizational charts show the formal leadership structure and the chain of command where roles, status, and responsibilities are clearly defined.

Informal leaders together with formal leaders are part of the shared vision of change. They are instrumental and critical to the change process since they are recognized by peers, often exhibit teacher leader qualities, and shape the school culture in positive ways. Informal leaders can be part of decision making so that a combination of top-down and bottom-up decisions are accepted and appropriate, depending on the nature of the change situation. Teacher leader roles and skills are part of participatory management as evidenced by the development of a collaborative school culture focused on student learning and continuous improvement.

In order to build the organization's capacity for change, the leader needs to consider when to assign or seek volunteers within the school to assume specific tasks. Recognizing knowledgeable and talented individuals who are ready to accept new roles can lead to opportunities for career advancement, recognition, and diverse perspectives. This creates a shared leadership model that develops change leaders for the future.

Since there is no one way to lead change, understanding various leadership roles and models can help change management. When possible, the effective change leader does not work alone, but rather distributes leadership to others through the assignment of specific tasks and the creation of change teams. The process of team building establishes collegiality and structured opportunities for formal and informal leaders to work together in achieving common goals for school improvement.

CASE STUDY

You are a teacher in a school that has experienced a tremendous decline in academic achievement over the last six years. Data indicate that test scores are failing, discipline infractions are rising, and parents are dissatisfied with the operations and management of the school. As a result, the principal is perceived as an ineffective leader. Even though the principal has been at the school for the last six years, faculty are unwilling and unsure as to how to address these problems in order to establish a shared leadership approach to implement changes that will improve the school.

The superintendent and the board of education have announced that the principal's contract will not be renewed at the end of the school year, and they seek input from faculty to establish the criteria and process for a new principal search. To begin the process, a review of current efforts to bring about change is advised. Because you are viewed as a teacher leader, you have decided to organize your peers, elicit their input, and make recommendations to the superintendent so that a quality leader who can address the needs of students, teachers, staff, parents, and the community can be identified and hired to bring change to the school.

EXERCISES AND DISCUSSION QUESTIONS

1. Describe your current school leadership structure by referring to the *Change Leadership Development Model* (figure 2.1). Identify the formal and informal leaders. Explain how people are assigned to tasks, and why teachers do or do not volunteer to serve on committees or take on other duties to help improve the school. Identify what isn't working to develop a shared leadership approach and suggest ways a new principal could engage others in improving the school.
2. Explain the various roles a change leader principal has to assume in leading the school and what qualities are needed to address the issues of student achievement, disciplinary infractions, and parental complaints. Give examples of the current principal's leadership style that are not effective, and what the faculty perceives is needed for effective leadership in the new candidate.
3. Create a rationale that explains the skills and dispositions the new principal will need to manage and lead the school toward improvement. Recommend when situational, moral, transformational, and servant leadership approaches are appropriate to address the vision of the school and the needs for improvement.
4. Review the organizational chart in your district and explain the division of labor between district and building level leadership. Create a short memo you would give to a principal candidate to explain the bureaucratic organizational system, the chain of command, and any ongoing efforts to instill participatory management that supports the needs of the school.
5. Since you are a teacher leader in an informal role, draft a job description that you would share with the superintendent to create formal teacher leader positions in the major content areas. Explain the seven domains of teacher leadership and how this model can support the new principal.

6. Your colleagues want you to stress the need for shared decision making with the new principal. Explain what it is, when it is appropriate, and what type of change leader the new principal should be to engage in shared decision making with both informal and formal leaders.
7. Explain to the superintendent the sources of power that exist in the school, and how these power structures will impact faculty support, buy-in, and loyalty to a new principal.
8. Describe individual and collective efficacy and how change leaders (both formal and informal) believe the school can improve with the support and understanding of the superintendent and the school board.
9. List rewards that are based on Herzberg's theory of motivation that will motivate faculty and staff and create the conditions to support school improvement led by the new principal.
10. Describe the composition of a change team and construct a process to identify the correct faculty and staff to serve on it.
11. Finalize your recommendations in a memo to the superintendent and school board, prioritizing the most essential knowledge, skills, and dispositions the new principal should possess in order to effectively lead change and improvement in your school.

REFERENCES

Bandura, A. (1997). *Self-efficacy: The exercise of control.* New York: Freeman.

Covery, S. (1991). *Principle-centered leadership.* New York: Simon & Schuster.

Cutajar, M. (2010). Max Weber bureaucracy theory. Retrieved from http://suite101.com/article/max-weber-bureaucracy-theory-a267433.

Elmore, R. (Spring 2000). *Building a new structure for school leadership.* Albert Shanker Institute.

Evans, R. (1996). *The human side of school change.* San Francisco: Jossey-Bass.

Fullan, M. (2001). *Leading in a culture of change.* San Francisco: Jossey-Bass.

Fullan, M. (2007). *The true meaning of educational change* (4th ed.). New York: Teachers College Press.

Goffee, R., & Jones, G. (2000). Why should anyone be led by you? In *Leadership insights: 15 unique perspectives on effective leadership.* Harvard Business Review Article Collection (September–October), 45–52.

Goleman, D. (1995). *Emotional intelligence: Why it can matter more than IQ.* New York: Bantam Books.

Green, R. (2013). *Practicing the art of leadership: A problem-based approach to implementing the ISLLC standards* (4th ed). Upper Saddle River, NJ: Pearson.

Greenleaf, R. (2002). *Servant leadership: A journey into the nature of legitimate power and greatness* (25th anniversary ed.). Mahwah, NJ: Paulist Press.

Hamel, G. (2012). *What matters now: How to win in a world of relentless change, ferocious competition, and unstoppable innovation.* San Francisco: Jossey-Bass.

Hanover Research (2011). Retrieved from www.hanoverresearch.com/toolkit/pdf/Best%20 Practices%20for%20District%20Office%20Organizational%20Structures%20and%20 Change%20Management%20Processes-%20Membership.pdf.

Hersey, P., Blanchard, K., & Johnson, D. (2001). *Management of organizational behavior: Leading human resources.* Upper Saddle River, NJ: Prentice Hall.

Johnson, S. (2010). Union leaders and the generational divide. *Education Week, 29*(24), 30, 40.

Johnson, S., Donaldson, M., Munger, M., Papay, J., & Qazibash, E. (2009). Leading the local: Teachers union presidents chart their own course. *Peabody Journal of Education, 84,* 374–393. DOI: 10.1080/01619560902973605.

Northouse, P. (2010). *Leadership: Theory and practice* (5th ed.). Thousand Oaks, CA: Sage.

Owens, R., & Valesky, T. (2007). *Organizational behavior in education.* Boston, MA: Pearson Education.

Raffanti, M. A. (2008). Leaders "sitting beside" followers: A phenomenology of teacher leadership. *Journal of Ethnographic & Qualitative Research, 3,* 58–68.

Rosenberg, S., & Silva, E. (2012). Trending toward reform: Teachers speak on unions and the future of the profession. *Education Sector Reports.* Retrieved from www.educationsector .org/sites/default/files/publications/REPORT-TeacherSurvey3f.pdf.

Sergiovanni, T. (1992). *Moral leadership.* San Francisco: Jossey-Bass.

Spillane, J. (2005). Distributed leadership. *The Educational Forum.* Retrieved from http:// sdexter.net/courses/589/downloads/SpillaneLeadership05.pdf.

Teacher Leadership Exploratory Consortium. (2012). Teacher Leader Model Standards. Retrieved from www.teacherleaderstandards.org/downloads/TLS_Brochure_sm.pdf.

Trybus, M. (2001). "An exploratory study of the influence of the Illinois Partnership Academy model on teacher's self-reported effectiveness." Unpublished doctoral dissertation, Loyola University, Chicago, IL.

Trybus, M. (2011). Facing the challenge of change: Steps to becoming an effective leader. *The Delta Kappa Gamma Bulletin, International Journal for Professional Educators, 77*(3), 33–36.

Wynne, J. (2001). Teachers as leaders in education reform. *Eric Digest.* Retrieved from www .eric.ed.gov.

Chapter Three

Change Management Tools and Interventions

OBJECTIVES

At the conclusion of this chapter you will be able to:

1. Understand principles and strategies of change management (ELCC 2.1, 3.1, 3.2, 3.3, ISLLC 2, 3).
2. Understand change management models (ELCC 3.1, 3.2, 3.3, ISLLC 3).
3. Describe strategies for leading school-wide change (ELCC 3.1, 3.2, 3.3, ISLLC 3).
4. Apply strategies for group change interventions (ELCC 3.1, 3.2, 3.3, ISLLC 3).
5. Apply strategies for intergroup change (ELCC 3.2, 3.3, 6.1, ISLLC 3).
6. Develop a vision statement and implement a vision plan (ELCC 1.1, 1.3, ISLLC 1).

SCHOOL-WIDE CHANGE MODELS

School educators often want to make school improvements, but don't always know the best way to do it. The ability to develop and apply a suitable model for implementing school-wide improvement is critical for any change effort. School leaders should take a collaborative approach to school change to obtain input and commitment from all stakeholders (Cameron, 2010; Levin, 2010).

While school leaders have utilized various organizational models and *school improvement plans* (SIPs), they have often fallen short of expectations in providing meaningful institutional change (Angelides, 2010). However, with careful selection of a viable change intervention and a structured implementation plan, most change efforts can be successful.

Collaborative Process Intervention Model

One model that can be used is called the *Collaborative Process Intervention* (Tomal, 2010). This collaborative model is designed to help school leaders implement school change through a systematic approach that includes all stakeholders in the change process (see figure 3.1). This is a strategy that focuses on making meaningful organizational improvements through the involvement of all stakeholders (e.g., teachers, administrators, students, board members, parents, and community members) through shared decision making.

This model is based upon taking a problem-solving approach to identifying issues in need of improvement through a systematic process of data collection, leading to taking action for constructive school improvement. The model consists of a five-phase process of planning, assessing, executing, implementing, and evaluating.

It entails a comprehensive step-by-step process in working with all stakeholders of the school in bringing about meaningful change within the

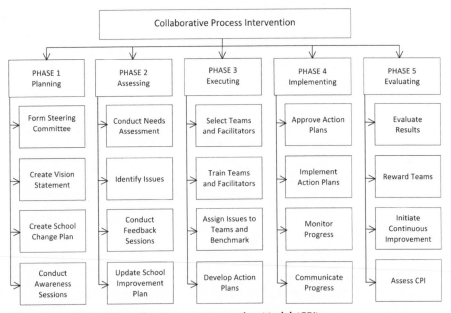

Figure 3.1.   The Collaborative Process Intervention Model (CPI)

organization. This process can be led by the school leader or in conjunction with an outside school consultant. The consultant can be useful in assisting school leaders with the change effort and can bring an independent, unbiased perspective to the team.

This first phase, *planning*, begins with the school leader developing a *steering committee* made up of various stakeholder representatives such as teachers, administrators, board members, parents, union representatives, and community members. The purpose of this committee is to understand the entire *Collaborative Process Intervention* (CPI) process, provide inspiration and direction for the change process, overcome roadblocks, maintain communications to all stakeholders, and provide resource support (e.g., finances, materials, facilities, and time).

The first goal of this phase is to develop a clear *vision statement* that reflects the needs of the students. This vision statement represents a crystallized long-range picture of what should be accomplished at the school. The development of the vision statement may require the use of one or more vision-building sessions to establish the vision and build interpersonal relationships and trust among the team members. The vision statement becomes the foundation for the ongoing process and helps everyone maintain a central focus while undertaking the continuous improvement process (Starr, 2011).

After the *vision statement* has been established, the steering committee should develop this statement into a *school change plan* that includes a general mission statement, and organizational goals that are aligned with district and state goals and outcomes. This school change plan also should be a comprehensive strategy for making school improvement.

An effective vision plan should include the vision statement, major goals, key strategies to accomplish the goals, performance indicators or metrics that describe the level of performance of key strategies, time frames, people involved in the process, roles of key individuals, and the general framework of the CPI process depending upon the extent of the desired change.

The school change plan can be independent of the *school improvement plan* (SIP), a revision of it, or an addendum to it, depending upon the needs of the school district. For example, if the school is in the beginning phases of developing the SIP then it probably makes sense to make the school change plan and the SIP one and the same. However, if the SIP has already been developed it may be sensible to revise the SIP based upon the CPI process.

Once the school change plan is completed, the steering committee should schedule *awareness sessions* for all stakeholders to explain the overall plan.

A letter describing the school change plan should be sent to all stakeholders. This communication process is a critical component in ensuring that everyone understands the collaborative process, expectations, and their roles in accomplishing the vision statement.

The purpose of phase two, *assessing*, is to clearly identify the school's strengths and areas in need of improvement (i.e., the major educational problems, gaps, and issues faced by the school). A needs assessment can cover areas such as curriculum and instruction, safety and security, communications, morale, technology, student transportation, facilities and resources, student centeredness, financial condition, work responsibilities, student performance, leadership, staff development, and parent and community involvement. This information can be collected through needs assessments, organizational surveys, employee interviews, school data, and analysis of student test scores.

An overall *needs assessment report* (i.e., the strengths and areas in need of improvement) should be prepared for the entire school. The change agent should be conscious to ensure anonymity and openness among the respondents. Some of the general areas in need of improvement might include: leadership, school policies and procedures, student performance, organizational climate, curriculum and instruction, learning resources, instruction, parent-community involvement, building and facilities, school environment, administrative and organizational structure, safety and security, school finances and allocation of funds.

Once the assessment report is prepared, a series of *feedback sessions* should be held to engage all stakeholders. The feedback sessions allow everyone to understand the results of the assessment, clarify issues, and allow participants to ask questions about the CPI process. A description of the next step in the CPI process can be included in the feedback sessions.

Once the feedback sessions have been held, the last step in phase two is to fully develop or revise the school improvement plan. Again, variations in this step can occur depending upon if the SIP is current or not. The information from the organizational assessment will provide valuable information for the school change plan and/or SIP.

The purpose of phase three, *executing*, is to address the areas in need of improvement identified in the assessment and implement the school change plan. *Action teams* should be assembled from various stakeholders from the school and community. Team members might consist of teachers, administrators, staff, parents, and concerned community members who are willing to work on a team in addressing areas in need of improvement and implementing the goals and key strategies.

The concept and intention of these teams are similar to *professional learning communities* (PLC) where all stakeholders can collaboratively work together in implementing the school change plan. Collaboration helps provide a synergistic approach to brainstorming, problem solving, and decision making during the executing phase.

Also, during this phase, several action teams can be established to work on the various issues such as policies, multiculturalism, finance, facilities, student achievement, parent and community relations, safety, transportation, curriculum and instruction, student discipline, human resources and organizational development, and technology.

The ideal size of an action team is about six to ten members. Each team should be responsible for addressing a specific issue as established in phase two. All teams should also be trained in *team building* and *group problem-solving* and *decision-making* strategies.

Each *action team* should consist of various stakeholders who genuinely desire to work on an issue, or who are associated with an issue by nature of their work responsibilities. For example, if the issue is to improve student discipline, the school disciplinary dean should logically be a member on this team. A listing of each team and issue can also be posted on the school website, where interested candidates can also sign up and people can review the teams' progress.

In addition to establishing action teams, a pool of *facilitators* can be created. These facilitators are typically stakeholders who are trained in group-processing techniques. Facilitators can act as group leaders in conducting the sessions and should not be members of the steering committee. They can also be valuable in keeping the action teams on task, developing the meeting agendas and minutes, and acting as a communication link with the steering committee and stakeholders of the school.

The facilitators can also post their teams' minutes on the school website so everyone can be kept informed of the teams' progress—a process called *score boarding* (a process that encourages transparency within an organization by allowing all concerned people access to view progress in achieving goals). Also it may be beneficial to match facilitators to a team with which they are not closely associated with the other team members or the issue, in order for them to remain neutral and maintain a focus on facilitating the session.

Once the teams and facilitators have been established, each team should be given information on the issue, and work should begin. In addition to using research literature to determine actions for the areas in need of improvement, the process of *benchmarking* should be encouraged (Camp, 1989).

This is a process of identifying the best practices of other schools which can be used as a basis for achieving greater performance. While the benchmarking process can be done continuously throughout the school year, the identification of suitable educational programs can be used to address solutions for the more immediate issues facing the school (Eadie, 2012).

The last step in the executing phase is *developing action plans.* Each action team prepares a detailed action plan for addressing the assigned issue. The steering committee might give each team a common format to use in preparing the action plan. For example, the format could include the issue titles, problem definitions, goals, actions, time frames, and rationales.

Phase four, *implementing,* consists of executing the actions. The action teams are not necessarily responsible for actually implementing the action plans. The final approval and overall implementation should be led by the school leaders. However, in some cases, the implementation of actions may be delegated to appropriate individuals or departments. For example, if a policies team develops a program for improving student discipline, the school discipline dean might logically be the person to lead the implementation of the program.

As actions are implemented they should be *monitored* and *progress communicated* to all stakeholders. The steering committee should develop a method to keep track of the progress of the actions and communicate the results to all stakeholders. Communication is critical to the process and it is easy for this step to be overlooked. Staff meetings, newsletters, department meetings, e-mails, blogs, news websites, parent letters, and special sessions are some of the communication methods that can be used.

The last phase, *evaluating,* consists of the action teams working with the appropriate stakeholders in evaluating the results of the actions. Follow-up surveys, individual and group interviews, student academic assessments, test scores, and benchmarking comparisons can be used as part of the process. This stage can be considered *data-driven decision making* to identify issues that need immediate correction and determine what actions require revision to meet the student learning and organizational needs.

Also it is important to include both formative and summative evaluations throughout the CPI implementing and evaluating phases. Evaluations during these phases can allow change agents to make adjustments early on rather than waiting until the end of the CPI process.

The teams should also be rewarded for their efforts and achievements. Various extrinsic reward systems such as letters of appreciation and luncheons can be used. The achievements of the students should also be celebrated through school events. Recognizing the students and including parents and community through school events can result in personal satisfaction and motivation for continued success.

The final steps involve *initiating continuous improvements* to the actions and assessing results. Also it is important to reward teams and reassess the entire CPI process and make necessary improvements. Results of actions should be documented and shared with all stakeholders. Based upon evaluation of the CPI process and outcomes, the steering committee may want to revise the process, rotate members to include fresh viewpoints, and allow others to participate in the process.

The CPI model can offer a viable process for implementing school-wide change and improvement. Variations of this model can easily be adapted for an organization based upon its unique needs and timing within the school year. While the process can be especially useful in developing the SIP for the ensuing year, it can also be valuable as an intervention process at any point in the school year.

Schools that are found to be in an educational crisis, facing potential closing, and experiencing chronic problems, and school leaders who do not know what to do, can utilize the CPI process as a catalyst to initiate viable change (Witt & Moccia, 2011). For example, if a school is suddenly put on the academic watch list and faces restructuring, the process could be utilized to reassess the school, develop a revised SIP, implement a modified plan, and take corrective action for improvement.

Action Research Model

Another model that can be useful for initiating school-wide change, or group change, is the *action research model* (see figure 3.2). In action research, the change agent is concerned with using a systematic process in solving educational problems and making improvements (Sales, Traver, & García, 2011). The change agent utilizes appropriate interventions to collect and analyze data and then to implement actions to address educational issues.

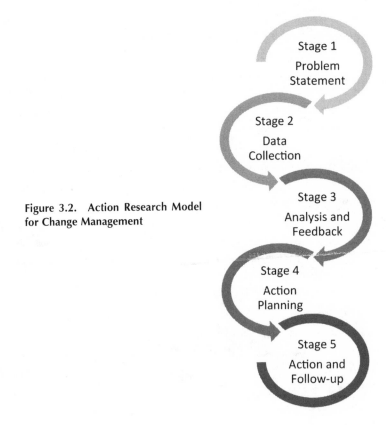

Figure 3.2. Action Research Model for Change Management

Action research is suitable for educators as a practical process because it generally does not require an elaborate process or complicated statistical analysis. Action research is direct in its purpose. Since the goal is to solve a given problem and make improvements, action research change agents rely less on scientific inquiry and inductive reasoning, and more on the practicality and feasibility of solving a given issue (Tomal, 2010).

Another feature of action research that makes it practical as a change strategy is the collaborative nature of the process. Generally, action research is conducted by a change agent (i.e., consultant, researcher, educator, or administrator) who works with school stakeholders within the context of a group (classroom, school, or organization) in conducting the intervention (Grundy, 1994).

The change agent acts as a catalyst in collecting data and then works with the group in a collaborative effort to develop actions to address the issues. Action research is often considered a change process as much as a research methodology. This process is concerned with the systematic collection of data, which is analyzed and fed back to the participants so that action plans can be systematically developed.

Therefore action research is distinguished from other change strategies because of the research-based, collaborative effort of the change agent in systematically working with the participants in developing action plans to make improvements. It also is a disciplined approach to data collection and decision making that is rooted in research methodology.

Before educators began using an action research model as a change strategy on a widespread basis, action research was utilized within the business world by organization development consultants. Organization consultants (OD change agents) have used action research principles to make operational and performance improvements within organizations (French & Bell, 1995). OD change agents have been generally concerned with improving employee morale, productivity, profitability, teamwork, communication, and quality of work life.

A final distinguishing feature of action research is the change agent's use of various interventions (i.e., set of structured activities), which provide the mechanism for the research action. These interventions include such techniques as team building, survey feedback, problem-solving strategies, intergroup activities, diagnostic assessments, interviews, role negotiations, conflict resolutions, third-party peacemaking, visioning, sociotechnical systems, statistical process controls, strategic planning, and a host of other creative schemes.

Understanding just a few of these interventions can allow the change agent to undertake meaningful school change efforts. Change agents should select an intervention that is most suitable for the problem and needs of the organization. Figure 3.3 illustrates some of the typical interventions used by OD consultants for various organizational problems.

The action research process begins with stage one where the change agent identifies the initial problem based upon a "felt need," or *problem statement.* For example, a school principal could conduct an initial diagnosis and conclude there is a need for teacher instructional development. The principal might explore different methods to collect data (e.g., survey, needs assessment) for determining skill deficiencies or areas in need of improvement for the faculty.

The principal would also conduct preliminary costs, time estimates, possible facilitators, tentative workshop dates, and other logistics prior to initiating and

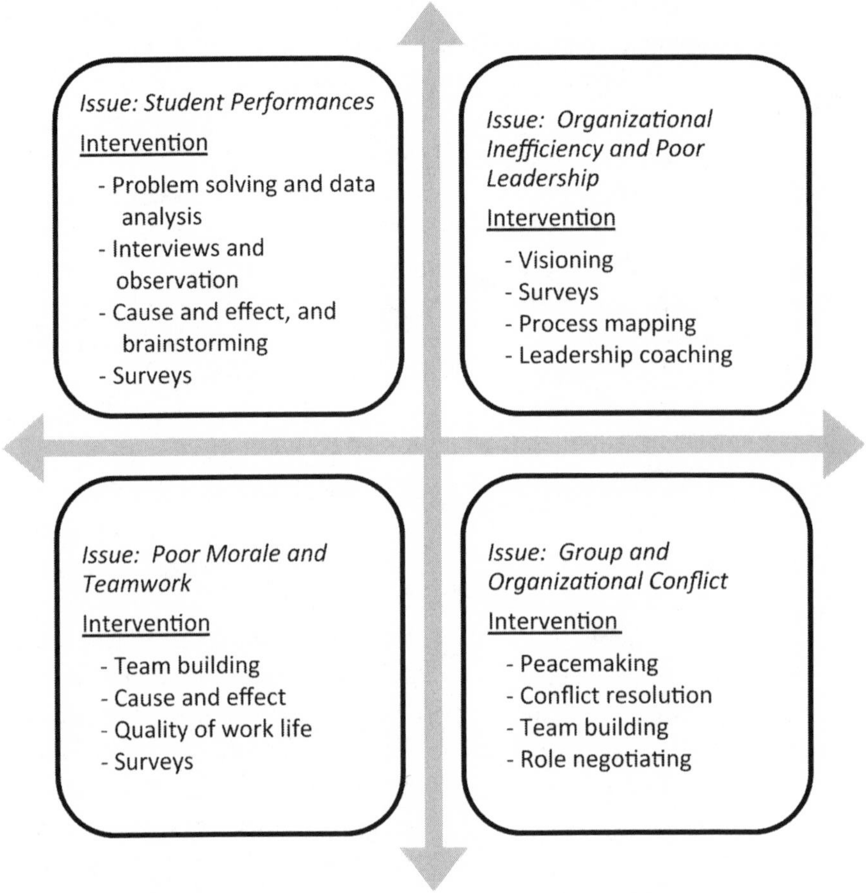

Figure 3.3.   Organizational Issues and Possible Intervention Method

announcing his or her intentions. It is important during this initial diagnosis stage that the principal conduct a reasonable amount of planning of resources such as time, people, and money to undertake the change process.

Data collection, the second stage, can be accomplished by several methods, such as: needs assessments, interviews, and group meetings. For example, if the principal elects to administer a needs assessment, confidentiality and anonymity should be ensured. A typical needs assessment might consist of a list of professional development topics (e.g., class management, learning styles, curriculum development, differentiated instruction, and instructional techniques), where the respondents are asked to assign a value to each topic (i.e., Likert Scale) indicating the degree of need for further development.

Random one-on-one follow-up interviews with teachers could also be conducted to gain clarification about the topics identified in the needs assessment period. This information could be helpful in gaining additional information concerning additional organizational issues and isolating specific development needs for the teachers.

Stage three consists of *analysis and feedback*. In this stage the principal analyzes the results of the survey and could calculate simple mean averages and then rank the professional development topics in order of importance. The principal could then conduct a feedback session with the faculty to review the rankings, gain clarification about the results, and obtain their input on the desired topics.

Although preliminary action planning might occur in this feedback session, the primary objective is to gain clarification about the collected data. Also, as a practical matter, various organizational issues (e.g., time constraints, teacher schedules, and need for further analysis) could hinder the principal from making final actions or commitments without conducting the feedback session.

The feedback session is a crucial stage in an action research process that provides an element of collaboration. This stage also helps develop communications, trust, faculty buy-in, and mutual support between the principal and faculty. The first three stages of the action research model (problem statement, data collection, and analysis and feedback) can be described as the problem-solving segment of the action research process. These stages serve to identify the cause(s) of the problem and specific areas in need of improvement.

Stage four, *action planning*, is the decision-making segment of the process. It involves deciding upon a course of action to address the issue(s). This process can be accomplished through a number of methods. The principal may determine the in-service training plans (i.e., final selection of topics, scheduling, and program logistics) to address improvement in student learning. A faculty involvement team, consisting of selected teachers, should also be assembled to develop and implement the action plans. Prior to implementing the actions, the final plan could also be reviewed by the entire faculty.

In stage five, the *action plan and follow-up* are implemented (i.e., in-service program). To reinforce a collaborative process, the principal might want to actually participate in the in-service program. This implementation stage represents the actual action part of the action research process. At the conclusion of the workshop, an evaluation should also be conducted to determine the extent to which training resulted in improved teaching and student learning.

A formal assessment should be conducted in the final stage, *evaluation and follow-up*. There should be timely and thorough follow-up in assessing the results that measure the action plan goals. Action research, unlike other models, includes implementation and evaluation as part of the process. For example, the principal might administer a workshop evaluation, conduct follow-up surveys, or measure actual benefits from in-service programs through student achievements, performance observations, etc. This stage could also act as a vehicle for continuous improvement for the school as it engages in the change process.

CONDUCTING INTERVIEWS

There are many group interventions that can be used to implement school change and improvements. It is important that the change agent select the appropriate intervention for the situation (Loesch, 2010). For example, if there is a need to collect input from a large group of participants, such as several hundred parents, it might be best to use a survey versus conducting one-on-one interviews. In other cases, small focus groups can be useful if more in-depth opinions are needed on an issue.

One of the most common interventions is the *interview*. Conducting interviews can be an effective technique for the change agent in getting detailed information on an issue. The interviewing process consists of asking questions to an individual or a group of participants and obtaining their verbal responses. The respondents should give their candid opinions, which are then directly recorded or paraphrased by the change agent.

Although the change agent is primarily concerned with getting verbal information from the respondents, valuable information can be made while observing their behavior to their responses that might not be obtained through the use of questionnaires. The interviewing technique also has the advantage of allowing the change agent to engage in an in-depth discussion with the respondents, which can often lead to more useful and richer information. Also the change agent can structure his or her questions based on specific areas of need that can elicit different types of responses.

There are some disadvantages in using the interviewing technique, such as time limitations, potential inaccuracy of interpretations of the participant

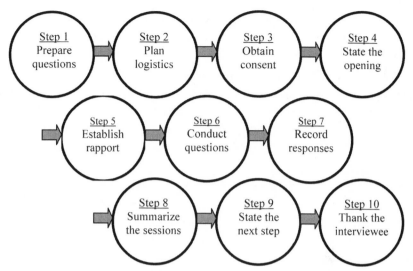

Figure 3.4.   Steps in Conducting an Interview

responses, difficulty in interviewing a large number of people, loss of anonymity, and individual feelings of discomfort in participating in the interviewing process. Regardless of whether the interviewer conducts a group
or individual session, the basic steps for conducting an interview are similar
and are listed in figure 3.4.

The first step in conducting the interview is to *prepare the questions*. The
questions should be tailored, based upon the information that the change
agent wants to obtain. Topics such as student learning, school climate, leadership, communications, curriculum and instruction, facilities, and safety
could be used. The change agent should also plan the *logistics* for the session, step two. It is important to find a suitable location where people feel
safe and comfortable to talk. This location should be in a quiet place with
little distractions or potential interruptions.

Step three includes obtaining a written consent form from the participants.
In some cases this may not be necessary if all the participants are adults,
understand the process, and voluntarily agree to participate. The fourth step
is the *opening*. Here the change agent needs to set the stage and explain the
purpose of the session and the ground rules such as: it is informal, questions
should be answered candidly and honestly, and stating the time allotted for
the interview.

Step five involves *establishing rapport* with the interviewees so that they feel
comfortable, not threatened, and will be more likely to share the information. It

is crucial that the change agent is always courteous and obtains trust of the interviewee. Without this trust, it is very difficult to obtain the desired information.

A simple approach in establishing rapport might be for the change agent to begin by simply asking the person how he or she feels about participating in the session. The change agent can then give his or her own feelings about past participation in interviews as a way to develop common ground. The change agent might also extend appreciation to the person for taking his or her time for the session and complimenting the person for participating in the session.

Step six consists of the interviewer *conducting the questions*. It is important that the change agent avoid asking leading questions (i.e., questions that bias the person's responses) so that the interviewee can give his or her candid responses without influence from the interviewer.

Open-ended questions are structured so that the interviewee is likely to respond with one or more statements. Examples include, "What do you like about the school?" and "What are the things that are hindering student achievement?" "What is your involvement in the school improvement process?" What is the perception of change in your school?" and "How is the school climate impacting change for improvement?"

Open-ended questions can be effective in obtaining a lot of information from the interviewee, although it can be ineffective and time consuming if the change agent is only concerned with obtaining a brief response. *Closed-ended questions* are best when the interviewer desires a brief "yes or no" answer. Typical closed-ended questions are: "Does the curriculum effectively improve student learning in reading?" and "Are teachers involved in designing effective safety measures to prevent bullying in the classroom?" "Do you like the safety program?"

The use of *paraphrasing* can be a useful questioning technique when the change agent desires the interviewee to elaborate. The paraphrasing technique consists of the change agent simply interpreting in his or her own words, as accurately as possible, what was heard. This reaffirms that the change agent was actively listening and was devoting full attention to the importance of the interviewee's opinions. This technique also helps draw out additional information and encourages the interviewee to keep talking.

Reflection is an interviewing technique that simply consists of a restatement of the interviewee's comment. For example, if the change agent states that he or she feels isolated in school, the change agent would simply respond by saying, "You feel isolated in the school?" Restatement techniques can force the person to continue talking and elaborate.

The use of the expanders, short words or expressions that the change agent can state, will cause the person to continue talking. Examples include "Go on," "I see," "Is that right?" "Okay," and "Good." The last technique, the use of *silence*, might appear ironic as a questioning technique, but sometimes the best questioning technique is to not ask a question at all. The use of silence can force the interviewee to begin talking and can be more useful in gaining information than asking structured questions that could stifle the interviewee from freely talking.

Step seven consists of *recording the responses* to the questions. The comments can be written verbatim or paraphrased by the change agent. A predesigned template comprising the categories of questions, or actual questions to discuss, can be helpful to the change agent in guiding the discussion and recording summary notes in a consistent and organized manner.

Steps eight and nine consist of *summarizing the session* and stating the *next step* in the process. The change agent might state that the next part of the process is to write a report and then present it to the school administrators. The last step (step ten) of the process is the *closing*. The change agent should *thank the interviewee* for participating in the interview.

There are several unique aspects in conducting a *group interview*. It is important to select people who can make a contribution to the interview session. Poorly selected people can interfere with the interviewing process and the change agent may fail to get useful results.

Conducting a group interview requires a great deal of skill by the interviewer. He or she needs to be able to pay attention to all the participants of the group and ensure that everyone contributes. The change agent needs to have good facilitation skills in controlling the dominating individuals and drawing out responses from shy individuals.

There are several types of difficult participants in a group interview. The *excessive complainer* is the type of interviewee who takes advantage of the session by expressing his or her negative feelings. Complainers often get off topic and need to be controlled. They often see causes of their problems as being outside influences, such as fate or other people.

Therefore, when problems are encountered, the complainers are more apt to blame others than to accept any responsibility and understanding of the root cause of problems. In dealing with complainers, avoid creating an adversarial relationship. The change agent might start by paraphrasing or restatement expressions such as "Okay, I understand," or "Let me see if I can paraphrase this." However, the interviewer should always try to focus on the problem, possible solutions, and keep the session productive.

The *hostile interviewee* can be difficult to control. This individual is generally abrupt, abrasive, and emotional. The hostile person is not the most common type of interviewee, but certainly is one of the most difficult to manage. They generally have strong feelings about the way others should behave and there is often a noticeable degree of anger, negativity, and distortion of real facts.

It is essential that when dealing with a hostile interviewee the change agent does not develop an adversarial relationship. Giving direct eye contact, deescalating any conflict or negativity, avoiding being overly accommodating, and keeping the session focused on the problem and solutions are key strategies to use.

The *long-winded interviewee* can disrupt the entire group by not allowing others to speak and often gives a biased view of the group's opinions. This person often comes across as a know-it-all. He or she is generally very confident and appears to have all the answers, and often generalizes about the problem from a biased viewpoint. In dealing with them, the change agent should make statements like, "I appreciate your responses, now can I hear other opinions, too?" Also the change agent can use paraphrase and restatement techniques to help control this dominating person.

The *shy interviewee* can be difficult to extract information from. This person often feels uncomfortable giving opinions in a group setting and might be hard to understand. He or she might have a sense of mistrust and feel embarrassed giving information in a group setting. Therefore in managing this type of person it is important to use open-ended questions, and paraphrasing and expander techniques.

The *drifter interviewee* is the type of person who takes discussion off track. This individual might focus on personal issues rather than the topic of the interview session. The change agent might want to take advantage of the session for hidden agendas or personal motives. In dealing with this type of person it is also important to redirect the individual to the topic and not reinforce this behavior.

Focus Groups

A special type of group interview is called a *focus group*. A focus group generally consists of about five to ten people, who are interviewed in a comfortable, nonthreatening setting. Although the change agent might ask questions to the focus group, the participants often just share their feelings and perception while the interviewer records their responses.

The focus group might also have an internal facilitator who helps to direct questions or record their responses. Sometimes responses can actually be recorded on a flip chart or newsprint. The interview questions can be placed on the top of several flip chart sheets and, when filled with responses, taped to the wall so that everyone can see the information.

Although there are different variations of conducting a focus group, the most common, from a change management standpoint, is to ask some general questions to the members and then record their responses. It is important to allow the participants to have freedom and responsibility for eliciting responses from everyone within their group.

The focus group operates best when all members have a common interest and are genuinely interested in obtaining everyone's views within the group. It also is important to select several participants for the group so that there are enough people to provide a representative sample but not too many to stifle discussion. In preparing questions for the focus group, the change agent should first develop a set of questions and then pilot the set of questions with experts to ensure that the questions are appropriate.

Defense Mechanisms

One of the potentially difficult aspects a change agent might encounter during an individual or group interview is defensiveness. When people become defensive, they often resort to using *defense mechanisms*. Defense mechanisms are psychological crutches that people utilize to prevent themselves from experiencing negative feelings.

Denial is a defense mechanism whereby people simply deny their own behaviors or feelings about a situation. For example, if a person is asked an uncomfortable question during the interview, he or she might give an untruthful response rather than experience potential embarrassment.

Projection is a technique where an individual transfers his or her feelings to another person. For example, a person might state, "I am not bad-mouthing the school, you are bad-mouthing the school," or "I'm not disorganized, you are disorganized." It is important for the change agent to watch for these patterns in people, which can give clues to their actual feelings and to ask follow-up questions to gain clarification or verification of their responses.

Reaction formation is a defense mechanism used when the interviewee states the total opposite of what he or she feels. For example, instead of stating that the person dislikes the school, he or she might say that school is great. This is a way to prevent the person from facing his or her true feelings and experiencing negative feelings. Change agents need to be aware of this defense mechanism and further probe the interviewee.

The use of *avoidance* is a very common technique whereby people simply avoid answering questions rather than face their true feelings. For example, nontenured teachers may not want to provide honest feelings about their own performance, or school leadership, for fear of the information getting to superiors and impacting their job security. During the interview session, a change agent might encounter aggressive behavior. In this situation, the change agent should be sure to establish rapport and always be courteous and respectful to the interviewee.

The use of *displacement* is a technique whereby a person blames another person or takes his or her negative feelings and transfers them to another person. The person might make statements such as, "I don't like my fellow colleague; she is always criticizing me." The person uses this technique to save face rather than take ownership for his or her own behavior. The change agent needs to keep the person on the topic and use closed-ended questions as necessary.

CONDUCTING SURVEYS

Conducting a *survey* is, without a doubt, one of the most popular and effective techniques for data collection in change management. A survey is used to obtain opinions from people regarding their feelings, beliefs, impressions, and facts about almost any educational issue or problem.

Although different formats are used in conducting a survey, the main objective is to ask questions directly to people to get information that can later be analyzed and then used to develop action plans to address educational issues. Although most surveys tend to be administered through a questionnaire to a large number of people, surveys can also be conducted on an individual basis and administered through the Internet, over the telephone, or in person.

Traditionally, surveys are used when there are a large number of people in the sample population and conducting personal interviews would be impractical and time consuming. This technique is called a *group survey*.

However, the use of the survey has evolved and is used for many different purposes, such as: surveying a person, school employees, teachers, parents, or all stakeholders of a school district.

For example, a change agent could administer a survey to assess the opinions of teachers regarding the use of a new reading instructional program. Actions for improving classroom practice could then be implemented and the teachers could take a follow-up survey to assess the results. Likewise a teacher could administer a survey to all of his or her students regarding class instruction. The teacher can then assess the students' opinions, implement actions to make instructional improvement, and then administer a follow-up survey to assess the results.

The process of conducting a survey should be systematic and thorough. Typical problems in conducting a survey consist of improperly defining the participants, neglecting to establish sufficient resources prior to starting the survey, failing to pilot the questionnaire, being too hasty in designing the items for the questionnaire, and having biased questions.

The steps in conducting a school survey are listed in figure 3.5. Step one in conducting a survey is *identifying the problem*. The change agent must first identify the educational problem and what needs to be improved. Generally this requires writing a well-defined statement of the problem. For example,

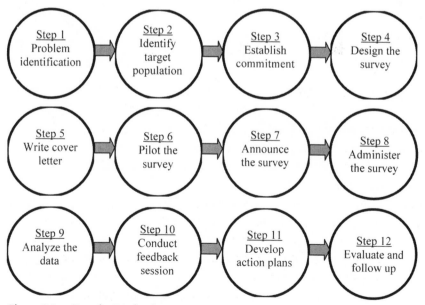

Figure 3.5. Steps in Conducting a Survey

the change agent might desire to improve the instructional skills of teachers, the math achievement of students, or the morale of teachers in a school.

This first step allows the change agent to decide on the actual objectives of the survey and determine if the survey is the best method for addressing the problem. In identifying the problem definition, some possible questions the change agent can ask include: "What is the educational problem?" "What is the intended outcome?" "Is the survey the best method for collecting information?" "Should another intervention method be used along with the questionnaire?" and "What is the time frame available to conduct the survey?"

Once the change agent has defined the problem, he or she must clearly *identify the target population* (step two). The exact participants to be included in the survey administration need to be identified. Understanding the target population and ensuring that the participants have the proficiency and knowledge to answer the items on the questionnaire is basic to all survey administration.

Step three consists of ensuring that there is *commitment* to conduct the survey. For example, a change agent might feel that a survey is the most appropriate intervention for collecting data, but resources are inadequate to administer it—such as enough people to distribute it, money for equipment and supplies, time for the teachers to complete it, time to analyze and share the results, adequate computer software, compensation for people, and time needed for the teachers to hear the results of the survey and participate in developing action plans.

It is also unrealistic to administer a survey during high-activity periods in the school year.

However, the change agent is more likely to gain administrator and teacher support to create, administer, and analyze the results of a survey if it is embedded as a component of the school improvement program. Therefore in establishing commitment, the change agent must consider all time frames, logistics, allocation of resources, and realistic goals and deadlines for the survey administration.

The *design of the survey* (step four) can be the trickiest part of the whole survey process. If the change agent doesn't develop a quality survey, the results of the survey will be poor. The actual survey, sometimes called the *instrument* or *questionnaire,* can be designed by using input from stakeholders built upon previous data collected and analyzed from other sources.

For example, if test scores show low performance in student reading performance, and it is evident that a concern regarding these results might be related to the lack of—or inappropriate—reading strategies, then a follow-up survey can target that area of need and go more deeply into questions that specifically address what types of strategies, and perhaps professional development, are needed for improvement.

Both open-ended questions and closed-ended questions can be used in the questionnaire. Closed-ended questions are similar to multiple-choice questions, which allow the respondent to select or rate a numerical value for the question. The answers to the questions typically measure the respondent's attitude, knowledge, or opinion.

Many different types of scales can be used for closed-ended questions. Selecting the best scale is crucial for allowing the respondent to easily answer each of the questions and for the change agent to later analyze the data. For example, if the change agent desires the respondent to make a forced decision among items that are similar, he or she might want to use the forced ranking scale.

A *forced-ranking scale* can be good to use to ensure that the respondent is forced into making a decision among several items. Of the many types of scales, the *Likert Scale*, named after Rensis Likert, is one of the more popular scales that use a five-point scale ranging from "strongly agree" to "strongly disagree."

Most *cover letters*, step five, should explain exactly the purpose of the survey, what will happen to the data, if names will be kept anonymous, and whether it is voluntary or not. The change agent needs to be concerned with any sensitive areas or politics in completing it. Therefore, before administering a survey, all potential concerns and issues in drafting the letter should be explained to ensure that the respondents will complete it with candidness and honesty.

A common mistake of change agents is their failure to properly *pilot the survey* before administering it (step six). For example, the survey can be pretested with a small, representative group of similar respondents. The change agent might conduct a focus group, read each statement aloud, and ask the respondents the meaning of each statement and if each statement reflects the intentions of the change agent. This process will help to establish the validity and reliability of the statements and allow the change agent to revise the statements as necessary.

In some situations, the change agent might want to *announce the administration of the survey* prior to actually distributing it (step seven). For example, if a principal is using a consultant to administer a school survey for all the teachers, announcing the survey a week in advance helps teachers be prepared to allocate the time for completing the survey and understand its purpose and importance.

The teachers also might need time to ask questions concerning the process prior to completing it. In other cases, when a teacher is administering a survey to a class of students, particularly if they are under eighteen, then a signed consent form from their parents is required. In some cases, it is not necessary to announce the survey, such as in a case of a department meeting, where a small group of teachers will complete a survey for the department chairperson.

In this situation, the chairperson could simply explain the purpose of the survey and then ask the teachers to complete it during the meeting, especially if it is a short questionnaire. In other cases, depending upon the time available, an Intranet survey can be useful, or an Internet survey using a commercial survey instrument. Figure 3.6 illustrates an example of a typical school survey.

Step eight consists of *administering the survey*. When the group is small, such as a department, then the sample population is considered self-contained and the change agent can easily administer the survey at one time and immediately collect them. The toughest part of administering the survey is when the group of participants is large.

Difficulty can arise when the participants are not at one location and the change agent needs to mail them. The use of mailed surveys almost always has a lower return rate. Also when electronic surveys are used via the Internet or Intranet, anonymity is lost and the return rate is often lower.

When there is a significantly large group of people, then the change agent may need assistants to help administer the surveys. For example, a change agent once administered a survey to two thousand parents whose children attended one large school. Rather than mail the surveys to all parents, given the postage expense and assuming the rate of return would most likely be lower, the change agent decided to use the students as a vehicle in administering the surveys to their parents. The change agent met with all the teachers from the school and gave clear directions for the teachers to explain to the students how their parents should complete the survey.

In this case, the survey process was called a *two-day survey turnaround*. All the teachers distributed the surveys to the students and the students immediately were told when they saw their parents to ask them to complete the survey without delay so that they could return the surveys by the next day.

Name of School: _____

Directions: Please indicate your group, then answer the following questions.
    Group #1: Grades 1–3   Group #2: Grades 4–5   Group #3: Grades 6–7

To what extent do you agree or disagree with the each statement? (sample questions)

1. School policies such as discipline and attendance are clearly stated and are fair.	5 Strongly Agree	4 Agree	3 Undecided	2 Disagree	1 Strongly Disagree
2. School policies and procedures are administered fairly and consistently enforced.	5 Strongly Agree	4 Agree	3 Undecided	2 Disagree	1 Strongly Disagree
3. I believe we are kept well informed on matters that affect us.	5 Strongly Agree	4 Agree	3 Undecided	2 Disagree	1 Strongly Disagree
4. Teachers' concerns are listened to and acted upon by administration.	5 Strongly Agree	4 Agree	3 Undecided	2 Disagree	1 Strongly Disagree
5. I believe students feel safe and are respected.	5 Strongly Agree	4 Agree	3 Undecided	2 Disagree	1 Strongly Disagree
6. Our school climate promotes student self-esteem and involvement.	5 Strongly Agree	4 Agree	3 Undecided	2 Disagree	1 Strongly Disagree
7. Teachers utilize effective instructional techniques.	5 Strongly Agree	4 Agree	3 Undecided	2 Disagree	1 Strongly Disagree
8. Teachers utilize adequate instructional resources.	5 Strongly Agree	4 Agree	3 Undecided	2 Disagree	1 Strongly Disagree
9. I feel the curriculum at our school is effective.	5 Strongly Agree	4 Agree	3 Undecided	2 Disagree	1 Strongly Disagree
10. I believe students are receiving a quality education at our school.	5 Strongly Agree	4 Agree	3 Undecided	2 Disagree	1 Strongly Disagree

Sample Open-Ended Questions

1. What are the things you like best about our school?

2. What are the things you like least about our school, and how can we improve them?

Figure 3.6. Partial Copy of a School Survey

Two days were allowed to complete this process, which was found to be more efficient than giving parents a greater length of time.

The change agent also allowed an additional week for any parents who were out of town or had extenuating circumstances in order to complete the survey. Teachers were also instructed to keep a list of all the students whose parents returned the surveys so that the researcher would know how by many people and from which classes surveys were completed in order to have a checks-and-balances system to ensure a credible process.

Undoubtedly every change agent is faced with *nonrespondents* who do not complete the survey. Extenuating circumstances often occur to prevent a participant from responding in a timely fashion. For example, participants might be absent, on vacation, or preoccupied with other activities and the change agent needs to follow up with these people. It is important to allow a reasonable amount of time to follow up with nonrespondents to obtain the highest rate of return. The change agent needs to make a professional judgment about whether to continue the study, if the rate of return appears to be too low.

Another important concern for the change agent is administering a survey to participants when the group is too small. A change agent might administer a survey to all the teachers within a school and the analysis might be calculated on departments; if a department has a small number of teachers, anonymity would be compromised. One general rule in conducting organizational surveys is that a department should have at least five members in order to ensure a minimum degree of anonymity. Otherwise, if the group is too small, the group might need to be combined with another group.

Step nine consists of *analyzing the data* from the surveys. Special features can be employed in designing and administering the questionnaire that will make later analysis easier. The survey can be administered to subgroups according to grade level, and statements can be designed to reflect the organizational issues in the school. A five-point Likert Scale is generally used to ask the participants their extent of agreement with each statement.

The statements in this school survey can also be categorized by *dimensions* (sometimes called *headings*). For example, the first two statements refer to the topic of policies (figure 3.7). Therefore dimension number one

Dimension	Questions
Dimension #1: Policies	Questions #1–2
Dimension #2: Communications	Questions #3–4
Dimension #3: Student-centered learning	Questions #5–6
Dimension #4: Instruction and resources	Questions #6–8
Dimension #5: Curriculum	Questions #9–10
Dimension #6: Organizational climate	Questions #11–12
Dimension #7: Parent and community involvement	Questions #13–14
Dimension #8: Work performance	Questions #15–16
Dimension #9: Miscellaneous	Questions #17–20

Figure 3.7. Dimensions of a School Survey

is labeled "policies." The third and fourth questions pertain to the topic of communications. The fifth and sixth questions pertain to "student-centered learning." The other dimensions are instruction and resources, curriculum, organizational climate, etc. Chapter 4 goes into greater detail in analyzing surveys, needs assessments, and school data.

Step ten consists of *conducting the feedback session*. Given that the intervention is a collaborative process, this step allows the participants to maintain involvement in the process. Generally, during the feedback session, the participants ask questions and learn about the results of the survey, but do not actually develop action plans until a later time. The feedback session is considered an opportunity for clarification and there is not sufficient time for action planning.

In some instances a feedback session might not be sensible or practical. For example, if a teacher administers a survey to his or her students, it might not be necessary to inform the students of the results. The results might be useful for the teacher in making action plans if the teacher feels that the results of the survey are too sensitive or simply not useful for them.

In most cases, if a change agent asks respondents to participate in a survey, they should have a right to know the results. For example, if a principal administers a school survey to all of his or her teachers, then it would seem logical that the teachers would get a copy of the results and would be involved in the development of action plans to address the issues.

The *development of action plans* to address the issues in a survey is step eleven. This process generally works best when done in a collaborative effort involving all participants. For example, if a survey were administered to parents, it might be wise to give the results of the survey to the parents and ask them to become part of the process of developing action plans. The action plans could be developed in a similar way as presented in the CPI process.

The last step of the survey process involves *evaluation and follow-up* (step twelve). Several approaches can be used to assess the results of the actions such as developing *smart* goals, performance indicators, analyzing student performance data, evaluating student test scores, and asking stakeholders for feedback. For example, a survey could be readministered to assess the effectiveness of the actions or follow-up interviews could be conducted.

If a school survey was administered to all the teachers, the change agent could follow up with the teachers at a six-month interval by holding department meetings to openly discuss the effectiveness of the survey process and the results of the actions that were implemented. Although the change agent might find it most useful to readminister the same survey, sometimes the availability of resources, such as time and money, can prevent administering the survey. However, administering a follow-up survey is essential, and sometimes required, for school improvement plans.

GROUP AND PROCESS INTERVENTIONS

Group and process interventions are data collection methods that are especially useful for analyzing school operations, teamwork, instruction, and educational programs. The objective of using these interventions is to facilitate group-structured sessions to brainstorm causes of problems that serve as a basis for decision making. The use of many of these techniques is an outgrowth from the *Total Quality Management initiative (TQM)*. TQM is a philosophy that embraces the idea of making continuous improvements to meet or exceed customer expectations (Herrington, 1987).

Six sigma, a common philosophy of TQM, is a data-driven approach to solving organizational problems and making improvements. It is a statistical term that represents 99.99966 percent in quality or only 3.4 defects per mil-

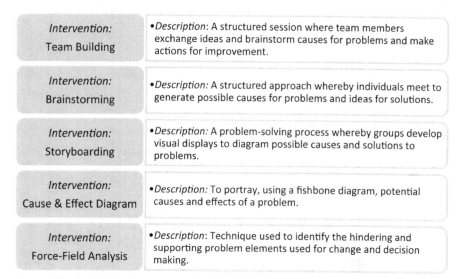

Intervention: Team Building	•*Description*: A structured session where team members exchange ideas and brainstorm causes for problems and make actions for improvement.
Intervention: Brainstorming	•*Description:* A structured approach whereby individuals meet to generate possible causes for problems and ideas for solutions.
Intervention: Storyboarding	•*Description:* A problem-solving process whereby groups develop visual displays to diagram possible causes and solutions to problems.
Intervention: Cause & Effect Diagram	•*Description:* To portray, using a fishbone diagram, potential causes and effects of a problem.
Intervention: Force-Field Analysis	•*Description*: Technique used to identify the hindering and supporting problem elements used for change and decision making.

Figure 3.8. Examples of Intervention Techniques for School Change

lion. Six sigma is also used as a belief of achieving the highest standards of performance, quality, and reliable processes, and near perfection.

For example, a company may strive for only three bad production parts per million, and a teacher may strive for only three mistakes per million in calculating students' grades. The concepts of TQM rely heavily upon the use of teamwork, problem-solving techniques, quality improvement, innovation and creativity, benchmarking, and customer satisfaction, which are all common elements of change management. Figure 3.8 describes several of these interventions.

The *team-building* session is a processing technique that can be helpful when a change agent desires to identify problems that affect an intact team. For example, a department chairperson who is experiencing problems within his or her department could assemble his or her staff and conduct a team-building session. In this session, the team members identify all the possible causes of problems that contribute to the department's performance.

Some of these possible causes include unclear goals, role incongruence, poor leadership, poor accountability, inadequate resources, or poor time management. These issues are often generated by a facilitator who lists all the possible issues freely identified by the members of the team. The group would then, by consensus, prioritize the issues that are most in need of improvement. Action plans are then developed to address the issues.

The *brainstorming* technique is another processing technique, and is similar to team building, but does not require an intact team. Brainstorming involves the pregeneration of ideas that cause problems. For example, a teacher working with his or her colleagues brainstorm a list of all the possible reasons for poor student achievement. During this freewheeling session, criticism is discouraged. The teacher acts as a facilitator and records all of the ideas on a flip chart or chalkboard, which are then later analyzed. Action plans are then made to address the issues.

One special type of group brainstorming is called the *nominal group technique* (NGT). This technique is an outgrowth of group brainstorming and uses a structured discussion by introducing a task or problem. The group then, often through use of index cards, produces a silent generation of solutions that are posted on a board or flip chart. The group then uses a series of round-robin discussions to clarify and evaluate the ideas and then select the best solution, which is often done through voting or ranking.

This technique can be especially good to use when the group wants to reduce the potential influence of an administrator or supervisor. Also it can be a useful technique when conflicts exist among the members of a group. Through this process, the team members can be more impartial and less likely to be critical of other team members.

Group problem-solving and decision-making intervention is a common technique that uses a structured approach in analyzing problems and determining solutions. Sometimes change agents attempt to solve problems based on proposed solutions without carefully isolating the root cause and they end up *treating the symptom versus the cause of a problem*. An analogy is taking an aspirin for a headache instead of treating the cause of the headache.

The steps of problem solving and decision making consist of analyzing the situation, establishing a problem definition, gathering the facts, listing possible causes, determining the cause, generating possible solutions, selecting the best solution, and developing an action plan to implement the solution.

The *storyboarding technique* is a processing technique that is useful in producing a visual picture of processes and procedures. This technique was originally credited to Walt Disney in the early 1900s when he pinned completed drawings in sequence on studio walls so that the production crew could better visualize the animated story. The process of storyboarding can be useful to the change agent.

For example, a change agent might identify a school problem such as high teacher attrition, excessive student tardiness, or poor student reading-

Discipline	1st period class	2nd period class	3rd period class	4th period class	5th period class	6th period class
problem issue #1	problem issue #1	problem issue #1	problem issue #1	problem issue #1	problem issue #1	problem issue #1
problem issue #2	problem issue #2	problem issue #2	problem issue #2	problem issue #2	problem issue #2	problem issue #2
problem issue #3	problem issue #3	problem issue #3	problem issue #3	problem issue #3	problem issue #3	problem issue #3
problem issue #4	problem issue #4	problem issue #4	problem issue #4	problem issue #4	problem issue #4	problem issue #4

Figure 3.9. Storyboarding Process

test results. A group of teachers could be assembled to begin the process: identify the issue, and list different subtopics for the issue, called visual frames (school organization, parents, school leadership, rewards, safety and security, etc.).

They could then brainstorm possible causes under each subtopic using sticky cards on a wall, and repeating the process for generating solutions. The key to this process is to see the results on a board by using sticky note cards, or flip-chart sheets. The process also supports a collaborative method of brainstorming that is generally conducive to the educational environment (figure 3.9).

The *cause-and-effect diagram* is a processing method that is especially useful in identifying technical problems. This technique, often called the *fishbone diagram*, provides a pictorial method of breaking down central problems in an understandable diagram. The objective of this fishbone diagram is to list the *effect* and *causes* of a problem that can then later be used to make decisions for improvement (figure 3.10).

As another example, a change agent could identify the effect of "poor student academic achievement." He or she then could brainstorm with a group of teachers to identify the major categories of causes that may be contributing to the poor student achievement. These might consist of poor teaching, instructional methods, curriculum, and school climate. Each of these categories would represent the branches of the diagram (i.e., fishbone arrangement).

The group would then brainstorm specific causes for each of the major categories. For example, under the category of "school climate," possible causes might include poor teacher morale, excessive discipline incidents, unsafe school, poor facilities, and presence of gangs. Under the category of "teaching," possible causes might include inexperienced teachers, apathy, low motivation, poor teaching skills, and poor placement of teachers.

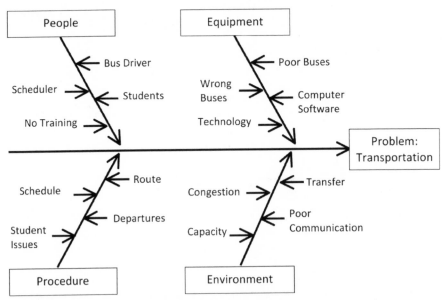

Figure 3.10. Example of Cause and Effect Diagram for Student Transportation Issue

The category called "instruction" could include lack of innovative instruction, outdated instructional techniques, poor facilities for instruction, and inadequate instructional resources. The last major category, "curriculum," might include outdated instructional materials, poor curricular resources, inadequate resource guides, and no alignment to standards. The number of major categories and their subcauses can vary, depending on the statement of the problem.

The *force-field analysis* intervention was first developed by Kurt Lewin (1943) as a group process for initiating change. The process involves identifying the *driving forces* (factors that promote change) and *restraining forces* (factors that hinder change). The result of these counterforces creates a polarization that prevents change from occurring (figure 3.11).

Lewin stated that in order to create change, the restraining forces must be reduced, the driving forces strengthened, or a combination of both. This technique can be useful for the change agent in identifying the restraining forces (causes of problems) that hinder effective change.

For example, if a teacher desires to improve reading skills, the force-field analysis technique could be used. The teacher could identify all the restraining forces that are hindering effective reading achievement, such as poor reading material, lack of parental support, low student motivation, inadequate reading resources, and poor reading-instruction techniques.

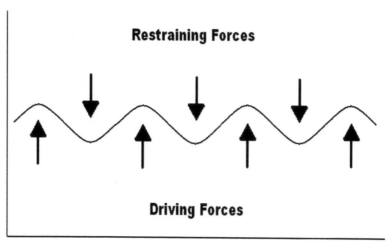

Figure 3.11. The Force-Field Analysis Technique

The driving forces could also be identified, such as the need to improve test scores, state mandates for reading improvements, and school district board policies. The teacher could use this technique as either an individual or group problem-solving process. Also, this technique can be used at any level within the school organization.

Process mapping is another technique that can be valuable in assessing work procedures, identifying inefficiencies, and taking corrective action. For example, if a school disciplinary dean desired to improve the student-discipline procedure, process mapping could be used. Each step of the discipline procedure could be outlined starting with the student offense, referral from the teacher, and so on. Figure 3.12 illustrates an example of the process-mapping procedure.

In this example, a group of educators could meet to outline all the steps and to identify any inefficiencies in the process, often referred to as *wastes*. Typical wastes might include too many forms, excessive steps, too much time between each step, method of communicating information, quality and mistakes in handling discipline, underutilization of people, too many people in the process, too much paperwork, inadequate technology, and so forth.

Once the inefficiencies have been identified, then the team needs to streamline the process by eliminating the wastes and making improvements. For example, the team may decide that there are too many hard-copy forms being used and a solution might be to reduce the number of forms, simplify them, and use a computer software program and database to manage the

1. Process Steps

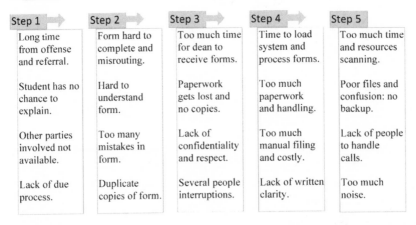

Step 1	Step 2	Step 3	Step 4	Step 5
Student discipline offense.	Teacher completes discipline form.	Send referral to school dean by school mail.	School dean reviews referral form.	School dean schedules conference.

2. Wastes

Step 1	Step 2	Step 3	Step 4	Step 5
Long time from offense and referral.	Form hard to complete and misrouting.	Too much time for dean to receive forms.	Time to load system and process forms.	Too much time and resources scanning.
Student has no chance to explain.	Hard to understand form.	Paperwork gets lost and no copies.	Too much paperwork and handling.	Poor files and confusion: no backup.
Other parties involved not available.	Too many mistakes in form.	Lack of confidentiality and respect.	Too much manual filing and costly.	Lack of people to handle calls.
Lack of due process.	Duplicate copies of form.	Several people interruptions.	Lack of written clarity.	Too much noise.

3. Action Plans: Action plans should be done to eliminate or reduce wastes and make improvements. All actions should include performance indicators/metrics.

Figure 3.12.   Process Mapping Example of the Partial Steps in Discipline Procedure

discipline process. Therefore process mapping is a valuable tool that can significantly contribute to improving school procedures and processes.

A technique that is very similar to process mapping is called *gap analysis*. This technique uses a method of outlining existing processes, identifying the existing state and the desired outcome, and then determining the "gap" between the existing and desired areas. A comparison of processes is often done side by side to identify the gaps. Once gaps are identified, actions are developed to improve the process, such as combining processes, improving the existing one, or replacing the existing one with a new process.

Another form of process mapping is *functional analysis*. This strategy uses a similar approach by selecting an activity or function to study, justifying the existence for the need of the activity, asking what would happen if it were eliminated, asking how it can be done another way, and brainstorming ways to improve the function. Finally, actions for improvement are then made, considering cost, quality, outcomes, and other benefits.

Groupthink

All change agents should keep in mind the negative effect of *groupthink* when using any group processing intervention. Groupthink, as theorized by Irving Janis (1972), suggests that group members try to minimize conflict and reach consensus without adequately analyzing and providing critical analysis in an effort to strive for unanimity. Essentially groupthink is a faulty decision-making process that can occur any time a group of members need to make a decision, especially when under stress, budgetary constraints, isolation, or time constraints (Janis, 1972).

The symptoms of groupthink may include illusions of invulnerability, rationalization, stereotyping, self-censorship, direct pressure, and illusions of unanimity among the group members. Therefore when working in group processes, the change agent should encourage critical evaluators, consider inviting outside experts into the sessions, thoroughly examine alternatives, and encourage independent thoughts and free opinions prior to rendering a group decision.

SUMMARY

The use of models, strategies, and interventions are critical elements of change management. Selecting the best change intervention for a given problem is a fundamental responsibility of the change agent. The use of *collaborative process interventions* and *action research models* can be useful for school-wide change initiatives.

The use of the *survey* is one of the more popular change-management tools. The survey can be used for small groups, large groups, and as an effective way to identify the issues of an organization. Processing tools are also useful, especially for small-group interventions. This method can help to identify wastes in an organization and provide a foundation for developing *action plans*.

Some of the more popular group and *process interventions* consist of team building, nominal group technique, problem solving and decision making, fishbone, gap analysis, functional analysis, and the force-field analysis technique. The use of process mapping can also be a valuable tool in assessing work procedures, identifying inefficiencies, and taking corrective action for improvement. The profession of a school leader calls for understanding and applying organizational development tools and interventions that can greatly contribute to school change and improvement. The more skills that a school leader can develop in using these techniques, the more likely it is that he or she will achieve meaningful school change.

CASE STUDY

You are a new principal at the Wakefield Public High School located in northwestern United States. On the first day of your job, the superintendent scheduled a meeting and presented you with several issues that currently exist at the school. Some of these consist of teacher and staff low morale, excessive parent complaints, high student disciplinary incidents, low student performance on standardized test scores, and high student absenteeism.

The superintendent has asked you to develop a *change-management proposal* to address these issues that can lead to developing viable actions for school improvement. Therefore develop this detailed proposal that includes a statement of the problem, list of change interventions to be used, and overall process of collaboration and communication with all stakeholders.

EXERCISES AND DISCUSSION QUESTIONS

1. Explain the *collaborative process intervention* model and how it can be used for school-wide change management. Suggest one or more variations of this model and rationale for the variations.
2. Explain *the action research* model and specific school issues that could be addressed by using this model.
3. List and describe the steps in *action research*, and suggest any variations that you feel could improve the model.
4. Show an example of the items in a survey that could be conducted at your school, based upon the survey model presented in this chapter.
5. Explain the different dimensions in categorizing the questions on an organizational survey.

6. List the typical stages in conducting an interview.
7. List several areas in need of improvement at your school, or school district, and what group and process interventions might be suitable to use.
8. Describe the *force-field analysis* technique.
9. Describe the *fishbone* technique.
10. Explain reasons why a change agent might select a survey versus conducting interviews.

REFERENCES

Angelides, P. (2010). The efficacy of small internal networks for improving schools. *School Leadership & Management, 30*(5), 451–467. DOI: 10.1080/13632434.2010.513169.

Cameron, D. (2010). Implementing a large-scale reform in secondary schools: The role of the consultant within England's Secondary National Strategy. *Journal of Education Policy, 25*(5), 605–624. DOI: 10.1080/02680931003749867.

Camp, R. (1989). *Benchmarking*. White Plains, NY: ASQC Quality Press.

Eadie, D. (2012). Getting out of the box. *American School Board Journal, 199*(1), 35–36.

French, W., & Bell, C. (1995). *Organization development*. Englewood Cliffs, NJ: Prentice Hall.

Grundy, S. (1994). Action research at the school level: Possibilities and problems. *Educational Action Research, 2*(1), 23–36.

Herrington, J. (1987). *The improvement process*. New York: McGraw-Hill.

Janis, I. (1972). *Victims of groupthink*. Boston: Houghton Mifflin.

Levin, B. (2010). The challenge of large-scale literacy improvement. *School Effectiveness & School Improvement, 21*(4), 359–376. DOI: 10.1080/09243453.2010.486589.

Loesch, P. (2010). 4 core strategies for implementing change. *Leadership, 39*(5), 28–31.

Sales, A., Traver, J., & García, R. (2011). Action research as a school-based strategy in intercultural professional development for teachers. *Teaching & Teacher Education, 27*(5), 911–919. DOI: 10.1016/j.tate.2011.03.002.

Starr, K. (2011). Principals and the politics of resistance to change. *Educational Management Administration & Leadership, 39*(6), 646–660. DOI: 10.1177/1741143211416390.

Tomal, D. (2010). *Action research for educators*. Lanham, MD: Rowman & Littlefield.

Witt, P., & Moccia, J. (2011). Surviving a school closing. *Educational Leadership, 68*(8), 54–57.

Chapter Four

Analyzing and Using Data for School Change

OBJECTIVES

At the conclusion of this chapter you will be able to:

1. Understand and use research data in change management (ELCC 3.2, 3.3, ISLLC 3).
2. Understand and interpret data and statistical analysis (ELCC 3.2, 3.3, ISLLC 3).
3. Describe various methods of displaying data and statistical information (ELCC 3.2, 3.3, ISLLC 3).
4. Understand how to interpret national, district, and local school data and report cards (ELCC 3.2, 3.3, ISLLC 3).
5. Apply data and statistical information for data-driven decision making (ELCC 3.2, 3.3, ISLLC 3).

UNDERSTANDING SOURCES OF DATA AND RESEARCH INFORMATION

The best way to make meaningful school change is to use research-based data and information in making leadership decisions. Nothing can be worse than educators recommending school change without any idea whether the actions have been supported through sound literature or practice by other school districts. *Research-based decision making* should be a fundamental requirement of all school leaders (Reeves & Flach, 2011).

One of the best sources of research data is educational research literature. A *review of the literature* should be conducted when considering most
school change initiatives. While conducting a literature search takes time, it
can have huge payoffs by avoiding ineffective or harmful school decisions.
The literature review can also introduce creative approaches to problems for
the change agent that might have been previously planned.

A literature search might include an extensive review of electronic databases, professional publications, journal articles, books, publications, and
personal interviews with expert professionals. Although a review of literature is essential in making student learning initiatives, it may be less important for making operational school changes such as transportation, technology, safety, and security, which often rely upon practices of other districts.

When conducting research literature reviews, there are two sources of information— primary and secondary. *Primary sources* are materials that are
written directly from the author.

Examples include dissertations, theses, or scholarly journal articles.
Secondary sources are written by someone else and are considered sec-
ondhand sources. Examples include books, magazines, or newspapers,
where the author reviews the primary work of the original author. Therefore primary sources are preferred since they are firsthand information and
generally of higher quality and reliability, whereas secondary sources are
subject to misinterpretations.

Electronic Databases

Most change agents should have access to a university or public library where
many excellent electronic databases are available. A popular database, called
EBSCO, provides abstract and full-text academic and school information that
can be exceptionally useful and quick to obtain by school change agents.

This database, produced by EBSCO Publishing, has about four hundred
full-text and secondary databases from journals, books, monographs, magazines, e-books, and digital archives. The company represents millions of
end users, especially elementary, high school, and university students, and
educators. EBSCO is easy to use, and once logged in, the prompts can be
followed to provide educational research on a host of topics.

There are other databases that can be helpful. *FirstSearch* is a popular
database that is a good source for educational articles, books, Internet sites,
archival materials, and research dissertations. It also provides abstracts and

full-text information and instant online access for school change agents who desire the latest research data and education information.

When searching research information in databases, there are many sources that can be used such as Internet and World Wide Web searches, indexes, books, technical papers, abstracts, original works, computer databases, journals, and professional handbooks. Typical educational sources include *The American Education Research Association, National Society for the Study of Education, Review of Research in Education,* and *The Handbook of Research on Teaching* and *Encyclopedia of Educational Research.*

One of the more popular research literature sources is the *Education Resources Information Center* (ERIC). This center contains a comprehensive online digital library of over one million bibliographic records such as scholarly journal articles, books, papers, software programs, reports, and works from associations and organizations. This center is sponsored by *The Institute of Education Sciences,* which is an agency of the *United States Department of Education.*

When using ERIC, a search can be conducted by entering bibliographic data such as the author, title of the work, and journal citation. Most of the materials can be obtained at no charge. Other helpful features of ERIC include basic and advanced search functions, thesaurus, and My ERIC, which allows the researcher to search and save the online information.

Benchmarking

Another source of school data and information is called *benchmarking.* Benchmarking is an outgrowth of the total quality movement and is a process of identifying the best practices of other organizations and adapting these practices as a basis for solving problems and making educational improvements. This technique can also be used as a quasi-literature search.

Benchmarking is similar to a literature review, except that it is less concerned with identifying academic and scholarly research publications and more concerned with identifying best practices. Identifying model programs of excellence based upon nationwide school practices can be a crucial component in making educational improvements. *Dantotsu,* a Japanese term, means "striving to be the best of the best," which is the essence of the benchmarking philosophy.

Several methods can be used in the benchmarking process. For example, if the goal is to improve student reading, the change agent could visit other school reading programs, contact outside universities and vendors, consult reading experts, attend professional association conferences, review magazines and journals on the subject.

The change agent might also assemble a team of fellow educators and each team could benchmark a different topic. This collaborative process could allow the benchmarking process to be conducted more efficiently. The members could later pool their findings for group discussion. The team could also collaborate in selecting the best method(s) to address the topic. Although benchmarking can be a valuable method, the process requires a commitment of time and human resources and the change agent needs to be willing to make this investment (Tomal, 2010).

Government and Professional Organization Websites

Another source of data and information is the use of government and professional organization websites. There many government and private educational organizations that post school data and information on websites, which can be a valuable source for educators. For example, the *National Center for Education Statistics* is a federal government agency that collects, analyzes, and reports numerous education data.

This website provides information on publications and products, surveys and programs, data and tools, school searches, education facts and news. Some of the programs include the *National Assessments of Adult Literacy* (NAAL), *Early Child Longitudinal Studies* (ECLS), *National Household Education Survey* (NHES), common core data (CCD), school district demographics, library statistics, common school standards, peer comparison tools, and school district profiles.

A source of educational statistics is the *American Institutes for Research*. This agency provides expert statistical analysis and reporting of school data. The agency also develops data-collection instruments, analyzes and interprets data, and writes reports, conducts studies, and posts this information for the public.

The *United States Department of Education* is one of the largest agencies of statistical and research data and information. This website contains information on education policies, funding, research facts and publications, best practices, grants, special education and rehabilitative services, and vocational education. The agency was created in 1980 and has over four thousand employees and a $68 billion budget.

Some of the major goals include establishing policies on financial aid for education, distribution of funds, collecting data on America's schools, disseminating research, addressing key educational issues, and prohibiting discrimination and ensuring equal access to education. However, the agency is dependent upon government budgets and can vary in the amount of detailed information or breakdown of the data (Aud et al., 2012).

There are many *professional* organizations that provide statistical educational data. Some of these include:

American Association of School Administrators (AASA)
American Educational Research Association (AERA)
Association for Supervision and Curriculum Development (ASCD)
Education Policy Analysis Archives
EDUCAUSE World Wide Web Server
International Reading Association (IRA)
International Society of Technology in Education (ISTE)
National Academy of Education (NAED)
National Association of Elementary School Principals (NAESP)
National Association of Secondary School Principals (NASSP)
National Association of State Boards of Education (NASBE)
National Education Association (NEA)

ANALYZING RESEARCH DATA
FOR THREATS TO VALIDITY

Regardless of the source of the data, it is critical that the change agent carefully analyze the source in terms of *validity* and *reliability* to ensure the information is relevant, valid, and applicable to the school. *Validity* refers to the extent to which the information is sound, useful, and well grounded.

Reliability is the extent to which information is dependable and consistently valid over time. Guarding against the many *threats to validity* is important to ensure that the data and information are relevant and valid for the change agent's school. Campbell and Stanley (1963) first established several threats to validity in 1963, which are summarized in figure 4.1.

The concept of *history* can have a negative effect upon data collection. *History* refers to the premise that many factors can affect the nature of data if collected at different points in time. Few things in life remain constant.

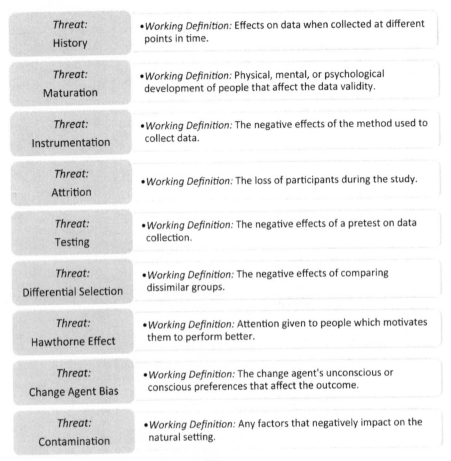

Threat: History	• *Working Definition:* Effects on data when collected at different points in time.
Threat: Maturation	• *Working Definition:* Physical, mental, or psychological development of people that affect the data validity.
Threat: Instrumentation	• *Working Definition:* The negative effects of the method used to collect data.
Threat: Attrition	• *Working Definition:* The loss of participants during the study.
Threat: Testing	• *Working Definition:* The negative effects of a pretest on data collection.
Threat: Differential Selection	• *Working Definition:* The negative effects of comparing dissimilar groups.
Threat: Hawthorne Effect	• *Working Definition:* Attention given to people which motivates them to perform better.
Threat: Change Agent Bias	• *Working Definition:* The change agent's unconscious or conscious preferences that affect the outcome.
Threat: Contamination	• *Working Definition:* Any factors that negatively impact on the natural setting.

Figure 4.1.   Examples of Threats to Validity

For example, if a change agent administers a morale survey to teachers, he or she most likely will obtain different results, depending upon which point in time during the school year it is administered.

If it is administered during midyear, the results may be different than if it is administered at year-end, just prior to summer vacation. Teachers may have more negative attitudes at the end of the school year than at midyear. Also, any number of factors can affect the data, such as world events, economic crises, policy changes, and traumatic events.

Another example of the impact of history on the validity of data is when an educator compares the school performance data from one year to another. While trends over time can be useful, making a comparison between one school year data and another may be invalid and may not reflect the true performance of the students if extraneous factors contributed to the results.

The school might have experienced a host of negative or positive factors in a particular year that could have influenced the results such as economic changes, a teachers' strike, administration turnover, policy changes, increase in neighborhood crime, higher student mobility, and facilities and environmental changes. The change agent should be careful to identify any factors that might impact the validity of the data reviewing research literature.

Maturation refers to the physical, mental, or psychological changes that occur in the participants. When researching elementary students, this factor is especially important because students in this age group are maturing at a quicker pace than in adulthood.

For example, if a change agent is collecting data in an attempt to observe the impact of a new teaching strategy, the positive gains might be caused by the mere fact that the students matured and not that the teaching strategy was more effective. To guard against this threat, the change agent might use another class as a *control group* for comparison (i.e., group that does not receive the new teaching strategy).

The term *instrumentation* refers to the method in which data are collected (e.g., survey, observation, interviews). The use of instrumentation, in itself, can impact the validity of the data being collected. For example, if a change agent is using the interview technique, it is possible that he or she might obtain more favorable responses simply because the respondent feels favorable toward the interviewer. Likewise, if the respondent dislikes the interviewer, more negative responses might be obtained.

The use of instrumentation might have a negative effect if the change agent selects the wrong type of instrument for collecting data. It is possible that a change agent might, under certain situations, obtain more favorable responses using an interview process than if he or she were to use a questionnaire. Respondents may be more likely to give more candid opinions through the use of an anonymous questionnaire than a personal interview.

The term *attrition* refers to the loss of participants during the data-collection process. For example, if a change agent is collecting student data over an extended time period and there are several student absences or attrition, the data will be affected. The change agent should monitor the attrition rate to ensure that there is a minimum loss of participants during data collection. Otherwise, if the attrition rate is too high, the change initiative should be abandoned.

A common practice in education is administering a pretest and posttest to students. If the tests are similar, the students might have learned enough from the pretest to show improvement on the posttest. This improvement might have nothing to do with the action administered, but rather simply because the students became *test wise*. To guard against this potential problem, the educator might eliminate the pretest, use different tests, or make sure a sufficient amount of time has elapsed before administering the posttest.

The term *differential selection* refers to a situation when two groups are dissimilar. For example, if a change agent administers action to one of two schools and then collects data on both schools for comparison, any differences can be explained because the two schools were different in the first place, not because the action was effective. In these types of situations, the change agent needs to be sure that the two schools are similar in characteristics such as age, academic ability, gender, behavior, socioeconomic status, and ethnicity.

The *Hawthorne Effect* refers to the fact that when people are given attention, such as through participation in a research study or a change interaction, they tend to be motivated to perform better. For example, if the change agent is showing the school board members a new curriculum program that is being used by teachers, the teachers' and students' performance might increase due to the fact that they are being observed, not necessarily because of the new curriculum program.

The *Hawthorne Effect* is a common phenomenon with newly employed school leaders. It is not unusual for the teachers and staff to be more motivated with a new principal at their school, but then, over time, their motivation level returns to the original state. This is called the *honeymoon stage* or a form of the *Hawthorne Effect* that suggests people's performance will increase for a short while with change, but in time will return to the original level. All educators, especially change agents, need to recognize and understand that any change may be short lived merely because of this phenomenon.

The term *change agent bias* indicates the unconscious or conscious preference for a positive or negative outcome of the change intervention. For example, if a change agent is administering a new learning program and hopes that the result will be positive, he or she might tend to unconsciously slant the results more positively. Although this bias can be intentional or unintentional, the results negatively affect the quality of the information collected and the outcome.

Therefore the change agent must maintain high standards of ethics and integrity and always try to be neutral and objective when implementing change interventions. Also, one way to help avoid this phenomenon is to make use of outside, independent consultants to maintain an unbiased perspective.

The term *contamination* refers to any factors that negatively impact the natural setting or actual data collection. For example, if a new instruction program is introduced by a teacher, and the principal observes the instruction, the results may be impacted by the principal's attendance. Many factors might contaminate a change intervention, such as unexpected interruptions, environmental conditions, lack of training, logistical issues, data-collection method, and skill of the change agents (Tomal, 2010).

UNDERSTANDING AND ANALYZING STATISTICAL DATA

A change agent does not need to be a statistician, but he or she needs to have a basic understanding of statistics to interpret research articles, test scores, and other student performance data. The first question that may be asked by the change agent is, "What types of data are important to examine when considering school change?" Figure 4.2 illustrates several categories of data that can be considered when improving a school.

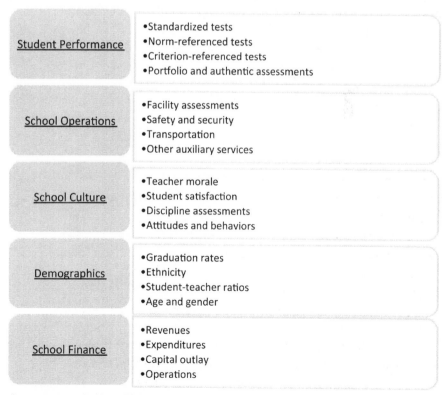

Figure 4.2.   **Examples of Measures of School Data**

Basic to school data are student performance outcomes, typically measured by standardized tests, norm and criterion assessments, and student authentic assessments (portfolios, etc.). Other data areas include school culture, school operations, student demographics, and school financial information. All these data areas can be helpful in examining current school conditions, implementing actions for school improvement, and establishing accountability practices (Monpas-Huber, 2010).

In reviewing school and student performance data a basic understanding of statistical terms is necessary. Figure 4.3 illustrates some of the common symbols and definition of terms used in statistical analysis. The mean, median, and mode are called *measures of central tendency*. The mean is simply the average score of a group of scores. The median, which reflects the midpoint of a set of scores, is often used to report teacher salaries or family income and is generally a better measure of central tendency than the mean score when the scores significantly vary.

The mode is the most frequent score of a set of scores. The mode represents the most common score, as opposed to a given midpoint or numerical average of a set of scores. Although it has limited value, it does allow a change agent to identify a common score from a group of scores, giving the change agent additional information in making interpretations.

Another term that is common to school data analysis is *measures of variability*. This term is a statistic that describes the dispersion, or spread, of the

Term or Symbol	Definition
Median	Middle score of a set of scores
$\bar{x}$ Mean	Mean, or arithmetic average
Mode	Most frequent score
Range of scores	Difference in the highest and lowest score
ΣX	Sigma (sum of scores)
(PR) Percentile rank	Percentage of students below a score
p	Probability or significance level (.10, .05, .01)
Variance	Dispersion of scores about the mean
(SD) Standard deviation	Measure of variance (68%, 95%, 99%)
NCE	Normal curve equivalent
Standards-based tests	Measures of state/federal standards
Standard score	Norm referenced distribution of scores

Figure 4.3. Definitions of Common Statistical Symbols and Terms

scores on a statistical curve. It is different from a measure of central tendency because, rather than representing a midpoint or an average score, it describes a measure of distance relative to the set of scores on a statistical curve.

Some terms used in association with measures of variability include the *range, variance,* and *standard deviation.* The *range* represents the difference from the lowest to the highest score in the group. It is often the measure of least reliability because its value can be affected by a single score that could extend significantly at the low or high end of the distribution. However, the range is still a good crude measure of checking the distribution of scores.

The term *variance* refers to the dispersion of the scores from the mean average. This measure can be useful in describing how much variation the scores have in relation to the average score. The most common statistic that is used to measure variance is called *standard deviation* (i.e., the variance of the scores).

There are three primary standard deviations used in statistics which are plus or minus one standard deviations, plus or minus two standard deviations, and plus or minus three standard deviations. In the normal curve, approximately 68 percent of the scores will be contained in the area between plus one and minus one standard deviation from the mean. Approximately 95 percent of the scores will be contained between plus and minus two standard deviations, and more than 99 percent will be included between plus and minus three standard deviations from the mean.

For example, if a group of student raw scores were plotted on the normal curve, it might represent a range from 70 to 130. The score of 70 would indicate the lowest-performing student and the score of 130 would represent the highest-performing student. The mean average of all the students would be 100.

Therefore, using the normal curve, approximately 68 percent of scores would be between 90 and 110. Ninety-five percent of scores would exist between 80 and 120, and more than 99 percent of the scores would be contained between 70 and 130. The use of *standard deviation* (SD) can be a valuable measure for change agents in interpreting student performance especially among several groups of students within the school district or as a comparison with other schools or groups of students in their state.

Understanding Significance Levels and Tests of Significance

Although complex statistics are not generally performed by change agents, having a basic understanding of *tests of significance* can help them interpret scholarly research and student statistical data. *Tests of significance* are used by statisticians to analyze school data to determine whether there is statistical significance. There are basically two types of tests of significance: *parametric* and *nonparametric,* depending upon the type of data being analyzed.

Once a set of data is analyzed using a test of significance, the statistician reports a significance level, or probability level (often called a "p value"). The most common significance level used in education is .05. This level means that there is a 95 percent chance that a true difference exists between an experimental group and a control group and not because of random chance (coincidence) or poor sampling.

Other significance levels used are .01 (or 99 percent confidence level), and .10 or (90 percent confidence level). The .01 significance level is a more stringent level and indicates that there is a 99 percent chance that there is a true difference between the two groups. Likewise, the .10 significance level would indicate that there is a 90 percent chance that there is a true difference between the two groups (a less stringent level).

Remember, the purpose of tests of significance is generally to accept or reject a hypothesis. Therefore when reviewing a scientific study, the change agent needs to see if there is significance. Often there is an asterisk (*) associated with the level of significance (e.g., null hypothesis is rejected).

There are many types of parametric and nonparametric tests of significance. For example, typical parametric tests of significance include a *simple t-test* (testing one group with a known population), *paired t-test* (testing one group under two conditions) *t-test for independent means* (testing two groups under one condition or treatment), and *Analysis of Variance* (ANOVA) (testing more than two groups under different conditions).

Some nonparametric tests of significance include Chi square (probability test, testing proportions in two or more groups), Sign test (two random variables or groups), Mann Whitney (two independent groups), Wilcoxon (matched paired groups), and Kruskal-Wallis test (three or more unmatched groups) which are associated with degrees of probability and have similar purposes as the parametric test of significance. Change agents don't need to be statisticians, but an understanding of statistics can help them interpret research-based studies.

An example of a test of significance is displayed in table 4.1. This example represents the output of applying a statistical *paired t-test* for two sets of student math scores (e.g., one class of students completing a math test and then the same group completing a second math test). The purpose

Table 4.1. Statistical Paired T-Test for Two Sets of Student Scores

Math 1	Math 2	t-Test: Paired Two Sample for Means		
80	89			
87	86		Math 1	Math 2
80	84	Mean	81.28571429	82.5
85	86	Variance	56.37362637	63.19231
90	96	Observations	14	14
70	74	Pearson Correlation	0.89314051	
68	68	Hypothesized Mean Difference	0	
78	75	df	13	
79	78	t Stat	−1.26252738	
80	83	P(T <= t) one-tail	0.114468702	
96	95	t Critical one-tail	1.770933383	
84	80	P(T <= t) two-tail	0.228937403	
86	85	t Critical two-tail	2.160368652	
75	76			

of this statistical test is to determine whether there is a significant difference in how the students performed in test one as compared to the second test or change initiative.

In interpreting the output in table 4.1 the headings of *math 1* and *math 2* represent the two sets of student scores. The mean, or average, of the scores is presented along with the variance. The observations (e.g., 14) indicate that there were fourteen students in the class who completed both math tests. The hypothesized mean difference is zero (0) which indicates a *null hypothesis*. The letters "df" refer to *degrees of freedom* and the formula is n − 1.

The change agent does not need to be concerned with the "df" number nor the remaining numbers other than the *two-tail p value* (0.229). This is the critical number in that it represents the *probability level* (significance level). In this case, .229 is higher than .05, and the change agent can see that there is no significant difference, *since the p value needs to be lower than .05 to be significant.*

Therefore, the change agent can conclude that there is no significance between how the students scored in the first math test as compared to the second math test. In this case, the change agent would probably want to examine the instruction between the two testing periods since there was no change in learning. Also, interpreting other types of significance tests can be made in this similar way. One good way to remember this point is using the expression "if the 'p' is low the null must go."

One of the more common uses of statistics for the change agent is interpreting national and state standardized test scores. Change agents, when reviewing school data, often rely upon national and state standardized tests to extract data and make comparisons. These tests generally include measures of central tendency, variability, and significance levels. In addition, most standardized tests report the percentiles and standard scores.

Standard scores are used so that students' performance on tests can be interpreted nationwide. Some common standard scores include stanine scores, z-scores, and t-scores. For example, the stanine score includes the numbers from one through nine, with five being the average. A stanine of five represents the fiftieth percentile of a set of scores in a distribution.

If a student were to score in the stanine of nine, this would indicate that the student has scored exceptionally high, in the very top end of the distribution (i.e., commonly called the *tail*). Likewise, if a student scored with a stanine one, this would indicate that the student performed very poorly and is in the lowest percentile of the distribution. Z-scores and t-scores are similar to stanine scores.

These tests are commonly used to calculate student test scores which are normalized to allow change agents to compare these scores with the general student population. The stanine scores are helpful to the change agent in identifying students who may need special services or instruction to advance to a higher stanine level.

Another term that is commonly used by many state boards of education is the *four performance standards* for determining student performance in reading, writing, mathematics, and science. Typical levels include: *exceeds standards* (advanced knowledge and skills), *meets standards* (proficient knowledge and skills), *below standards* (basic knowledge and skills with gaps in learning), and *academic warning* (limited learning with major gaps in learning). This system is a straightforward way of designating student performance and can be used to build student evaluation rubrics.

Interpreting Survey Questionnaires

Survey questionnaires are often used in school change efforts (Burns et al., 2011). Surveys typically include a standard *Likert Scale* in which the respon-

Variable: Q1, The School Climate Promotes Student Self-esteem

Mean = 2.79   SD = 1.13

	Value	Frequency	Cumulative Frequency	Percent	Cumulative Percent
Strongly Agree	1	2	2	6.25	6.25
Agree	2	13	15	40.63	46.88
Undecided	3	10	25	31.25	78.13
Disagree	4	5	30	15.63	93.75
Strongly Disagree	5	2	32	6.25	100.00

Figure 4.4.   Example of a School Survey Question Data Summary

dents indicate their extent of agreement by circling a value between one and five (strongly agree, agree, undecided, disagree, and strongly disagree).

After a survey has been administered, the results are generally tabulated and displayed on charts and graphs. Descriptive statistics, as explained in chapter 3, are often used to display the output. Figure 4.4 illustrates a typical data output for one question from a school survey.

For example, in figure 4.4, question number one pertains to the *extent of agreement* for student *self-esteem.* The mean for this item is 2.79, the standard deviation is 1.13, and the number of people (n) is 32. The total number and cumulative percentage for the respondents who responded favorably to this item is 15 (46.88 percent). As a change agent, this would be cause for concern. The change agent would then make an analysis that less than half of the teachers were positive toward their school in providing a climate that promotes student self-esteem.

Therefore the change agent would need to further investigate this question by talking with the respondents and gaining clarification to a negative response. As a rule, when interpreting data, a change agent would identify an *area in need of improvement* as any item that the majority of respondents did not rate positively.

If an item were to be positively viewed by the majority of respondents (e.g., two-thirds of the participants or more), then the change agent would conclude that this item is a *strength.* Although there are no absolute standards in which the change agent decides which items are a strength (i.e., positive item) or weakness (i.e., area in need of improvement), a general guideline includes: if more than 50 percent disagree or strongly disagree with an item, the issue should be identified as a concern, if two-thirds agree or strongly agree to an item, it is a strength.

Interpreting Research Studies

Change agents need to be able to interpret research studies and how they apply to the local school setting. Most quantitative research studies have statistical tables where conclusions are reported. A typical set of statistical data from a research study is illustrated in table 4.2. The results show a comparison of motivational factors between elementary and high school teachers. When interpreting this table, a comparison of the two groups can be made. It is apparent that groups feel that the most important factor for motivating students is *engaging instruction*.

Both high school and elementary school teachers have similar opinions regarding the importance of *engaging instruction*, and a change agent might surmise that the other factors are less important. Other motivational factors that were significantly different included *good school and classroom conditions*, students feeling *socially connected*, teacher *verbal appreciation* for good performance, using *tangible rewards*, and *good grades*.

By comparison, elementary school teachers feel that all these motivational factors are more important except for the use of good grades. The high school teachers ranked good grades as being much more important than elementary school teachers for motivating their students. The use of these data and tables are common practice for change agents, education consultants, and school leaders (Bernardt, 2005).

Table 4.2. Example of Research Results with Statistical Significance

Motivational Factors (n = 45)	Elementary Teachers			HS Teachers		
	Mean	Median	S.D.	Mean	Median	S.D.
Good school/class conditions	*6.45	7	2.41	8.20	8	1.64
Students feel socially connected	*7.43	8	1.82	8.55	9	2.30
Fair discipline by teachers	6.77	7	2.14	6.36	7	1.51
Teacher verbal appreciation	*5.29	5.5	2.0	6.45	6	.80
Tangible rewards (stickers, etc.)	**6.59	8	2.83	7.27	9	2.37
Good grades	*7.41	9	2.76	3.64	3	2.25
Teacher giving encouragement	3.91	4	1.80	3.64	3	.73
Teacher giving regular feedback	5.14	5	1.84	5.09	6	1.18
Providing engaging instruction	2.06	2	.90	2.0	2	.75
Ensure good class management	*3.71	4	1.95	5.81	4	3.25

* $p < .01$ ** $p < .05$

INTERPRETING NATIONAL, STATE, AND
LOCAL SCHOOL PERFORMANCE DATA

The *National Center for Education Statistics* (NCES) is one of the most useful sites to gain information on school data and statistics. It is the primary U.S. agency for collecting, analyzing, and disseminating education data. The mission of NCES is to serve "the research, education and other interested communities" (NCES, 2012). The *Office of the Commission* sets the policies and standards for this center and is responsible for the operation, statistical quality, and confidentiality of the data.

The agency disseminates the information through news releases, statistical reports, directories, data briefs, handbooks, and other publication reports on a regular basis. They publish three primary surveys called the *Digest of Education Statistics*, *Projections of Education Statistics*, and the *Condition of Education*. For instance, table 4.3 shows an example of elementary and secondary student enrollment and pupil-teacher ratios.

Among the publications and products produced by NCES are *Condition of Education in the United States*, *Digest of Education Statistics*, *High School Dropout and Completion Rates*, *School Crime and Safety*, in addition to numerous other publications. NCES also conducts a number of surveys and statistical analyses in areas of national assessments, early childhood, elementary and secondary education, international educational activities, data systems and core education standards, and common core of data (CCD). In addition, NCES provides periodic conferences and training, press releases, and live statistical chat conferences.

The NCES *Nation's Report Card in Mathematics* provides a detailed report of the results of the *National Assessment of Educational Progress* (NAEP) in mathematics at national grades four to eight. This study represents samples of over two hundred thousand fourth graders and nearly two hundred thousand eighth graders who participate in the mathematics study. The assessment results are compared to those of previous years and trend lines are established (Chen & NCES, 2011).

Another example of an NCES report card is the *Trial Urban District Assessments Results of Grades 4 and 8*. This report primarily focuses on the reading proficiency of fourth through eighth grade public school students

Table 4.3. Elementary and Secondary Schools—Teachers, Enrollment, and Pupil-Teacher Ratio: 1970 to 2009

Year	Teachers			Enrollment			Pupil-Teacher Ratio		
	Total	Public	Private	Total	Public	Private	Total	Public	Private
1970	2,292	2,059	233	51,257	45,894	5,363	22.4	22.3	23.0
1975	2,453	2,198	255	49,819	44,819	5,000	20.3	20.4	19.6
1980	2,485	2,184	301	46,208	40,877	5,331	18.6	18.7	17.7
1984	2,508	2,168	340	44,908	39,208	5,700	17.9	18.1	16.8
1985	2,549	2,206	343	44,979	39,442	5,557	17.6	17.9	16.2
1986	2,592	2,244	348	45,205	39,753	5,452	17.4	17.7	15.7
1987	2,631	2,279	352	45,487	40,008	5,479	17.3	17.6	15.6
1988	2,668	2,323	345	45,430	40,189	5,242	17.0	17.3	15.2
1989	2,713	2,357	356	45,741	40,543	5,198	17.0	17.2	15.7
1990	2,759	2,388	361	46,451	41,217	5,234	17.0	17.2	15.6
1991	2,797	2,432	365	47,728	42,047	5,681	17.1	17.3	15.6
1992	2,827	2,459	368	48,500	42,823	5,677	17.2	17.4	15.4
1993	2,874	2,504	370	49,133	43,465	5,668	17.1	17.4	15.3
1994[1]	2,925	2,552	373	49,898	44,111	5,787	17.1	17.3	15.5
1995	2,974	2,598	376	50,759	44,840	5,918	17.1	17.3	15.7
1996[1]	3,051	2,667	384	51,544	45,611	5,933	16.9	17.1	15.5
1997	3,138	2,746	391	52,971	46,127	5,944	16.6	16.8	15.2
1998[1]	3,230	2,830	400	52,525	46,539	5,988	16.3	16.4	15.0
1999	3,319	2,911	408	52,876	46,857	6,018	15.9	16.1	14.7
2000[1]	3,366	2,941	425	53,373	47,204	6,169	15.9	16.0	14.5
2001	3,440	3,000	441	53,992	47,672	6,320	15.7	15.9	14.3
2002[1]	3,476	3,034	442	54,403	48,183	6,220	15.7	15.9	14.1
2003	3,490	3,049	441	54,639	48,540	6,099	15.7	15.9	13.8
2004[1]	3,536	3,091	445	54,882	48,795	6,087	15.5	15.8	13.7
2005	3,593	3,143	450	55,187	49,113	6,073	15.4	15.6	13.5
2006[1]	3,622	3,166	456	55,307	49,316	5,991	15.3	15.6	13.2
2007	3,634	3,178	456	55,203	49,293	5,910	15.2	15.5	13.0
2008[1]	3,674	3,219	455	55,235	49,266	5,969	15.0	15.3	13.1
2009[2]	3,617	3,161	457	55,282	49,312	5,970	15.3	15.6	13.1

[In thousands (2,292 represents 2,292,000), except ratios. As of Fall. Dates are for full-time equivalent teachers. Based on surveys of state education agencies and private schools; see resource for details.]

[1]Private school numbers are estimated based on data from the Private School Universe Survey.
[2]Projection. Source: U.S. National Center for Education Statistics. *Digest of Education Statistics,* annual, and *Projections of Educational Statistics.* See also www.nces.ed.gov/annuals.

who are from large urban districts in the United States. This report provides significant data and comparisons from those of previous years on the reading assessment scores for both fourth and eighth graders in five districts. It also includes scores for lower-income students in six districts and an overall average score for both higher- and lower-income students (NCES, 2010).

The NCES *Educational Technology in U.S. Public Schools* (2010) is a useful report on national technology use in public elementary and secondary schools. The basis of this report originates from a survey of public schools and the use of information technology in classrooms and schools. This information can be helpful for change agents in comparing these national data with their own school (Gray et al., 2010).

Another worthwhile NCES report is the *Trends in High School Dropout and Completion Rates in the United States* (Chapman et al., 2011). This report shows trends in dropout and completion rates of public high schools in the United States. The data are classified by race and ethnicity, sex, age, family income, disability, and geographic region.

The report shows comparisons among black, Hispanic, and white students, and dropout rates by family income, low-income student dropout rates, and other trends and data comparisons. This information can be useful for all change agents in establishing benchmarks and comparisons with their own schools.

Besides providing data for student performance, another popular NCES report is the *Revenues and Expenditures for Public Elementary and Secondary Education* (Cornman, Noel, & NCES, 2011). This information can be helpful for change agents in comparing the fiscal condition of their school with other districts in the country.

This report contains the *common core of data* (CCD) which is an annual collection of elementary and secondary public education data based upon finance surveys conducted throughout the United States. The report also provides revenues and expenditures of schools and includes regular, special, and vocational education, and charter schools.

NCES provides data for specific programs as well, such as a report on *Arts Education in Public Elementary and Secondary Schools*. In this report a survey of students' access to arts education and the quality of instruction are provided. Some of the areas included in this report are professional development activities, teaching loads, instructional practices of elementary and secondary teachers, music specialists, and individual arts specialists.

The study includes issues and data concerning availability of curriculum-based arts education and other areas such as dance, drama, and theatre. It should be noted that the information provided in this report is based upon self-reporting data by school officials.

Analyzing National School Data

Understanding standardized student performance data can be a grueling exercise for any change agent. There are numerous sources for standardized

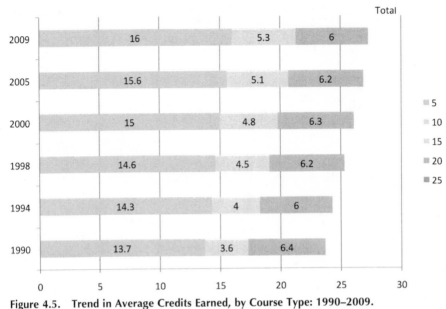

Figure 4.5.   Trend in Average Credits Earned, by Course Type: 1990–2009.

Source: U.S. Department of Education, Institute of Education Sciences, National Center for Education Statistics, High School Transcript Study (HSTS), various years, 1990–2009.

student data such as federal (National Center for Education Statistics), state department of education, local school district data, university, and private education organizations.

Figure 4.5 illustrates national data on trends in average credits earned by high school students. Notice in this chart that the data are being reported for a period between 1990 and 2009. It also displays the total course credits for core academic courses and other academic courses. This is a typical bar chart that allows the change agents to easily view and analyze the data, which can be helpful in comparing the information to the agents' own school data.

The chart information is based on high school transcript study of credits earned for three types of courses: core academic, academic, and other courses. The core academic courses are defined as English, mathematics, science, and social studies. Academic courses are defined as fine arts, foreign languages, and computer-related studies. The last category of other courses includes areas such as vocational education, personal health, and physical education (Keaton & NCES, 2012).

In addition to student performance data, other national school information is available and can be useful for making school operational improvements. For example, table 4.4 illustrates information on school facilities. This table illustrates the percentage of distribution of elementary and secondary public

Table 4.4.   Percentage Distribution of Public Elementary and Secondary Schools: Environmental Factors on Instruction in School Buildings

Environmental Factor, by Building	None	Minor	Moderate	Major	N/A
Permanent buildings					
All Factors Taken Together	56	33	9	1	—
Artificial lighting	76	18	5	1	—
Natural lighting	73	18	5	1	3
Heating	63	24	10	3	1
Air conditioning	46	21	10	6	17
Ventilation	66	22	8	3	—
Indoor air quality	69	21	7	3	—
Acoustics or noise control	61	27	9	3	—
Physical condition of ceilings, floors, walls, windows, doors	71	19	8	3	—
Size or configuration of rooms	64	23	9	4	—
Portable buildings					
All Factors Taken Together	5	30	13	2	—
Artificial lighting	68	25	5	3	—
Natural lighting	62	26	7	1	4
Heating	66	23	7	2	1
Air conditioning	63	22	7	4	3
Ventilation	62	24	11	3	—
Indoor air quality	62	26	10	2	—
Acoustics or noise control	56	26	14	4	—
Physical condition of ceilings, floors, walls, windows, doors	60	26	11	3	—
Size or configuration of rooms	5	26	11	5	—

SOURCE: U.S. Department of Education, National Center for Education Statistics. (2007). *Public School Principals Report on Their School Facilities: Fall 2005* (NCES 2007–007).

schools, indicating the extent to which various environmental factors interfered with the ability of the school to deliver instruction in school buildings by type of building.

Typical environmental factors include lighting, heating, and air conditioning, ventilation, air quality, and noise control. This information can be used by change agents to assess their own school facilities and environmental conditions, and make comparisons with national statistics. There are many environmentally conscious people today and the use of this information can be valuable for educators in improving the school surroundings.

Analyzing State School Data

Most states have fairly common school reporting, often called the *State School Report Card*. For example, table 4.5 shows data for the state of New

Table 4.5. Example of State Report Card Data Environment

Length of School Day	
Amount of time school is in session on a normal school day.	
School	6 hours: 30 minutes
State Average	6 hours: 30 minutes

Instructional Time	
Amount of time per day students are engaged in instructional activities.	
School	5 hours: 30 minutes
State Average	5 hours: 43 minutes

Student/Computer Ratio		
Number of students per instructional computer.		
	School	*State Average*
2010–11	4.1	3.6

Student Performance Indicators

New Jersey Assessment of Skills and Knowledge
LANGUAGE ARTS LITERACY

Level	Year	Number Tested	Proficiency Percentages		
			Partial	*Proficient*	*Advanced*
School	2010–11	62	16.1%	62.9%	21%
	2009–10	68	25%	61.8%	13.2%
District	2010–11	815	20.2%	65%	14.7%
	2009–10	832	19.8%	63.9%	16.2%
DFG	2010–11	13364	27.7%	62.8%	9.5%
	2009–10	13761	31%	61.5%	7.5%
State	2010–11	99951	36.9%	56%	7.2%
	2009–10	101435	40.2%	54.2%	5.6%

SOURCE: State of New Jersey, Department of Education.

Jersey's State Report Card. These data include the school environment, length of school day, instructional time, and student-to-computer ratio.

For example, the length of the school day is six hours and thirty minutes in one school, which is the same as the state average. The instructional time, of five hours and thirty minutes, demonstrates that this school's instructional time is below the state average of five hours and forty-three minutes.

Likewise, the number of students per instructional, multimedia-capable computer provides a ratio of 4:1 for this specific school as compared to 3:6 for the state average. Table 4.5 also shows the assessment of skills and knowledge for language arts literacy.

As illustrated in the table, data is provided at the school, district, DFG, and state levels. Proficiency percentages are provided and categorized by partial, proficient, and advanced, as well as the number of students tested.

In addition to the sample data illustrated in table 4.5, state report cards include a myriad of other information such as enrollment by grade level, average class size, Internet connectivity, numbers of computers and locations, students with disabilities, limited English proficient (LEP) data, language diversity, and student mobility rates. Statistical data on student performance in areas such as mathematics, language arts literacy, and reading are often included.

Besides student data, the state report card often includes information on total revenues, expenditures for education, number of institutions, population demographics, and characteristics of elementary and secondary schools. As an example, table 4.6 illustrates data for the state of California.

This table, provided by NCES (2011), shows the scores in math, reading, science, and writing for the state of California and the average schools in the United States. This type of chart is especially useful in showing the comparisons between states and U.S. averages, as a way of benchmarking data for student performance (Nabors-Olah, Lawrence, & Riggan, 2010).

Table 4.6.   State of California Sample Profile

Progress	California	U.S. (Avg.)
Scale Score, Grade 4 Math	232	239
Scale Score, Grade 8 Math	270	282
Scale Score, Grade 4 Reading	209	220
Scale Score, Grade 8 Reading	251	261
Scale Score, Grade 4 Science	137	149
Scale Score, Grade 8 Science	136	147
Scale Score, Grade 4 Writing	146	153
Scale Score, Grade 8 Writing	148	154

SOURCE: National Center for Educational Statistics, 2011.

Analyzing School District Data

Most school districts use a common school reporting summary, often called the *District Report Card*, which is similar to the state report card. For example, table 4.7 shows the typical fiscal information for a school district, in this case, Chicago Public Schools. The chart provides detailed information

Table 4.7. **Example of School District Data**

CHICAGO PUBLIC SCHOOLS			
(2010–2011 School Year; Fiscal Data from 2008–2009)			
County: Cook County	County ID: 17031		
Grade Span: (Grades Pre-K–12)	Total Schools:		648
	Total Students:		407,157
	Classroom Teachers (FTE):		24,760.33
	Student/Teacher Radio:		16.44
	ELL (formerly LEP) Students:		51,992
	Students with IEPs:		51,739
	Amount	*Amount Per Student*	*Percent*
Total Revenue:	$5,028,161,000	$11,931	
Federal:	$1,182,403,000	$2,806	24%
Local:	$2,332,938,000	$5,536	46%
State:	$1,512,820,000	$3,590	30%
Total Expenditures:	$5,543,642,000	$3,154	
Total Current Expenditures:	$4,602,119,000	$10,920	
Instructional Expenditures:	$2,730,872,000	$6,480	59%
Student and Staff Support:	$593,546,000	$1,408	13%
Administration:	$551,823,000	$1,309	12%
Operations, Food Service, Other:	$725,878,000	$1,722	16%
Total Capital Outlay:	$649,521,000	$1,541	
Construction:	$630,555,000	$1,496	
Total Non-El–Sec Education & Other:	$76,895,000	$182	
Interest on Debt:	$215,007,000	$510	

SOURCE: NCES.ed.gov/ccd/district search

on the total number of schools, students, and teachers. In addition, the total revenue, including federal, local, and state, and expenditures are provided. A useful statistic is the actual percentage of the sources of revenue as well as the expenditures (Johnson et al., 2011).

A change agent can use this information to compare with other districts to make data-driven decisions for the school district. School board members also can find this information valuable as well. Like the state school report card, other information contained in school district data would include information on the school demographics, student performance, and other information as outlined in the state report card.

Analyzing Local School Building Data

The data at the local school level are often provided for specific school buildings as well as the school district. Typically data for a school building are compared with the district and state data in a school report card. Many states provide academic excellence awards which can be good goals for local schools to strive to obtain. For example, figure 4.6 illustrates an example of local school data. This first part of the table illustrates the average ACT composite score for the local school students and growth as compared to state average.

The second part of figure 4.6 provides an example of an Illinois school standardized test called the *Prairie State Achievement Examination* (PSAE). This is a test that measures the achievement of students in grade eleven in the areas of reading, mathematics, and science. Typically it is a two-day standardized test, whereby high school juniors take the PSAE along with the ACT exam.

In addition, the state of Illinois uses the *Illinois Standards Achievement Test* (ISAT) which measures the achievement of students in reading and mathematics in grades three through eight and in science in grades four through seven. This test is written to correlate with the state and national common core standards which represent what students should know and be able to do. The data in figure 4.6 provide 2010 ISAT and PSAE math scores for grades three through eleven and the percentage meeting or exceeding standards.

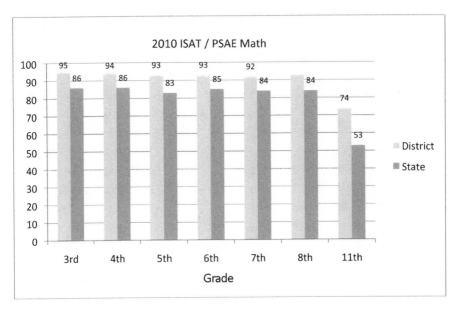

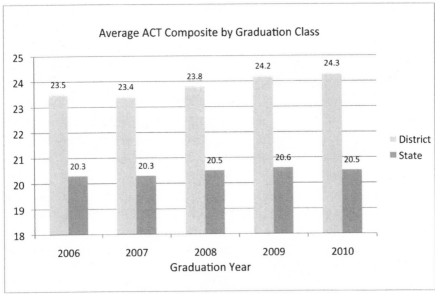

Figure 4.6. Example of Local School Data on Student Performance

SUMMARY

The analysis and use of data and research information is a fundamental task for change agents in making data-driven decisions. Some of these sources include electronic databases, benchmarking, government and professional organizations and websites, and private educational agencies. All change agents need to understand common *threats to validity* in interpreting research studies and information and the relevancy to their own school.

Some of these threats include history, maturation, instrumentation, attrition, differential selection, the *Hawthorne Effect,* contamination, and bias. Just because a change effort worked in one school doesn't mean that it will work in another school. Nor just because a research study has been reported in a journal, is it relevant or valid to use for another school.

The ability to understand and interpret statistical data is a prerequisite of all change agents. Some of the common statistical terms include measures of central tendency, measures of variability, standard deviation, significance levels, and parametric and nonparametric tests of significance. While the change agent does not need to be a statistician, he or she needs to fundamentally understand these terms and how they are used when interpreting statistical data such as standardized test scores, research studies, and national and state school report cards.

Another important aspect in·making school change is the reliance on national, state, district, and local school data and information to make an informed decision. The use of the *National Center for Education Statistics* is a valuable site that can provide enormous information for school change initiatives.

For example, this agency reports information on student standardized scores, financial information, facilities, student credits, and common core standards which can be compared to other schools' data and national data information. The role of the change agent is one that can have a profound impact on students, and their decisions need to be done with good judgment and well-grounded research.

CASE STUDY

You are an assistant principal at the Southfield Public High School. You have been asked to serve on a school improvement task force to examine the current student performance and environment of the school. Your task group needs to present a comprehensive proposal on making a school-wide change on all aspects of the school.

The new principal and superintendent, supported by the school board, would like your task group to develop several components in the proposal such as: What data should you examine? What outside research and information will you base your recommendations on? What national, state, district, and local school data might you find useful in making your recommendations? And what other relevant items would you include?

EXERCISES AND DISCUSSION QUESTIONS

1. Explain the different sources for obtaining school data and research information.
2. Explain the term *benchmarking* and how it can be used in making meaningful school change.
3. Describe the various data and educational information provided by the *United States Department of Education*.
4. List and describe several *threats to validity* in analyzing research data.
5. List and explain several statistical terms and definitions common to educational research literature and student performance data.
6. Explain the purpose of *tests of significance* and how they are used in educational research.
7. Describe examples of information by NCES.
8. Explain the value of providing *standard deviation* and how a change agent could use this information in making analyses in a school district.
9. Analyze your school report card and make inferences as compared to state and national school performance.
10. Explain what data other than standardized test scores could be important for a change agent in making conclusions for school change.

REFERENCES

Aud, S., Hussar, W., Johnson, F., Kena, G., Roth, E., Manning, E., & National Center for Education Statistics. (2012). *The condition of education 2012*. NCES 2012-045. National Center for Education Statistics.

Bernardt, V. (2005). Data tools for school improvement. *Educational Leadership, 62*(5), 66–69.

Burns, S., Wang, X., Henning, A., & National Center for Education Statistics. (2011). *NCES handbook of survey methods*. NCES 2011-609. National Center for Education Statistics.

Campbell, D., & Stanley, J. (1963). *Experimental and quasi-experimental designs in research.* Chicago: Rand McNally.

Chapman, C., Laird, J., Ifill, N., Kewal Ramani, A., & National Center for Education Statistics. (2011). *Trends in high school dropout and completion rates in the United States: 1972–2009.* Compendium Report. NCES 2012-006. National Center for Education Statistics.

Chen, C., & National Center for Education Statistics. (2011). *Numbers and types of public elementary and secondary schools from the common core of data: School year 2009–10.* First Look. NCES 2011-345. National Center for Education Statistics.

Cornman, S., Noel, A., & National Center for Education Statistics. (2011). *Revenues and expenditures for public elementary and secondary school districts: School year 2008–09 (Fiscal Year 2009).* First Look. NCES 2012-313. National Center for Education Statistics.

Geijsel, F., Kruger, M., & Sleegers, P. C. (2010). Data feedback for school improvement: The role of researchers and school leaders. *Australian Educational Researcher, 37*(2), 59–75.

Gray, L., Thomas, N., Lewis, L., & National Center for Education Statistics. (2010). *Educational technology in U.S. public schools: Fall 2008.* First Look. NCES 2010-034.

Johnson, F., Zhou, L., Nakamoto, N., & National Center for Education Statistics. (2011). *Revenues and expenditures for public elementary and secondary education: School year 2008–09 (Fiscal Year 2009).* First Look. NCES 2011-329.

Keaton, P., & National Center for Education Statistics. (2012). *Numbers and types of public elementary and secondary schools from the common core of data: School year 2010–11.* First Look. NCES 2012-325. National Center for Education Statistics.

Monpas-Huber, J. (2010). Explaining teachers' instructional use of state assessment data: A multilevel study of high school teachers in Washington state. *Journal of School Leadership, 20*(2), 208–237.

Nabors-Olah, L., Lawrence, N., & Riggan, M. (2010). Learning to learn from benchmark assessment data: How teachers analyze results. *Peabody Journal of Education, 85*(2), 226–245.

National Center for Education Statistics. (2010). *The nation's report card: Grade 12 reading and mathematics 2009. National and pilots state results.* National Assessment of Educational Progress. NCES 2011-455. National Center for Education Statistics.

National Center for Education Statistics. (2011). *The nation's report card: Reading 2011. Trial urban district assessment results at grades 4 and 8.* NCES 2012–455.

National Center for Education Statistics. (2012). nces.ed.gov.

Reeves, D., & Flach, T. (2011). Data: Meaningful analysis can rescue schools from drowning in data. *Journal of Staff Development, 32*(4), 34–38.

Tomal, D. (2010). *Action research for educators.* Lanham, MD: Rowman & Littlefield.

Chapter Five

Implementing Change: Resource Management

OBJECTIVES

At the conclusion of this chapter you will be able to:

1. Understand the steps for the *School Change Resource Implementation Model* (ELCC 3.1, 3.2, 3.4, 4.2, 5.4, ISLLC 3, 4, 5).
2. Articulate the obstacles in implementing change (ELCC 3.1, 3.2, ISLLC 3).
3. Describe how managing resources is a national challenge (ELCC 3.1, 3.2, 4.2, 6.3, ISLLC 3, 4, 6).
4. Describe the relationship between educational resources and achievement (ELCC 3.1, 3.2, 3.4, 4.2, 5.4, ISLLC 3, 5).
5. Understand what education resources are and why they are important in promoting change (ELCC 3.1, 3.2, 3.4, 4.2, 5.4, ISLLC 3, 4, 5).
6. Identify how the allocation of resources can promote change (ELCC 3.1, 3.2, 3.5, 6.2, ISLLC 3, 6).
7. Understand how to evaluate the effectiveness of change (ELCC 3.1, 3.2, 3.4, 4.2, 5.4, 6.2, ISLLC 3, 4, 5, 6).

THE SCHOOL CHANGE
RESOURCE IMPLEMENTATION MODEL

Implementing successful school change requires the alignment, acquisition, and allocation of resources. Depending upon the nature of the change or problem, the management of the resources will vary. For example, state versus federal funding, in-house expertise versus consultants, tangible versus intangible resources, etc. The initiation of change can come from many sources (see discussion on drivers in chapter 1). It can be a result of a legal requirement such as change in state or federal law, board of education goals, strategic planning, staff initiatives, parental concerns, demographic changes, or a change in available financial resources.

Entrepreneurship is the most complex form of change. It often requires scores of ideas before one is selected. It encourages the acceptance of ideas that may seem ridiculous at times. It involves looking for new relationships, paradigms, and links. It requires investors and, most importantly, it requires risk. Do change agents do this in education? Peter Drucker said that "innovation is the specific tool of entrepreneurs, the means by which they exploit change as an opportunity for a different business or a different service" (Drucker, 1985, p. 19).

Can school change agents exploit change in education? Can we, as change agents, take the initiative? Can school change agents engage in uncertainty? For the entrepreneur it is all about ideas, benchmarking, capital, and a business plan. Not all that different than what we do in education. So, maybe what we need to be successful in education is a few *edu-entrepreneurs* (Schilling, 2006).

Edu-entrepreneurs are school change agents who adapt an entrepreneurial paradigm in making meaningful school change. Whatever the reason or source of change, an organization must recognize it and decide to address it. The key to the successful implementation of change at any level in a school system is to have a process.

There are many existing models for school change, data gathering, and statistical evaluation as described in earlier chapters. Most of these focus on schools and school systems. However, often they don't emphasize the most important ingredient—*resources*. Prior to proposing a model for implementing school change, an examination of a few key concepts from the private sector needs to be done. For example, in the private sector everything usually starts with a business plan. The purpose of a business plan is to identify:

1. The opportunity
2. Target market
3. Competitive advantages
4. Financials
5. The team
6. Resource strategies

These basic components of a business plan really aren't all that different from the change process in schools except for the fact that schools aren't in the business of making a profit. Schools are in the business of educating students. So the terms may vary, but the basic goals of efficiency and effectiveness are the same.

Schools should seek changes that are effective and efficient if at all possible. Change in either the private or school environments begs the question, "Would you invest in this idea?" In other words, is there some intrinsic or extrinsic reason that this idea is good for students? Intrinsic reasons would include student motivation and achievement, citizenship, compassion, ethics, etc. Extrinsic reasons would include competitiveness, standardized tests, class rank, etc.

Change can also be the impetus for efficiency. In the private sector, customers are "king." In schools, the focus is on students. Whether private or public, organizations should utilize change as a motivator for repurposing resources from noncore functions to core functions. By definition noncore functions would be those operations of the school that do not directly impact instruction such as food services, cleaning, transportation, safety, and security. Core functions are those that directly relate to instruction such as classroom teachers and aides. Figure 5.1 shows a typical Model for Implementing Change in the Private Sector.

Looking at figure 5.1 there are several decision points in the private sector process. The same is true in the education sector. Each step in the change process is a building block on the next one. Problems at one stage may lead the organization to readjust or reevaluate earlier steps. Like the business sector, there are a number of steps in the process for implementing change in schools. Figure 5.2 shows the *School Change Resource Implementation Model.*

Following is a description of each of the steps:

Identify the need or opportunity. The first step in the School Change Resource Implementation Model is to identify and define the need or opportunity. This is no different than the process a doctoral student goes through in picking a topic for a dissertation. First, the student has to identify a research topic and then operationally define it. In a school or school system this could be simply looking for cause-and-effect scenarios. For example, students who receive low reading comprehension test scores may be an indication of lack of adequate vocabulary skills.

The opportunity is to increase reading comprehension scores by addressing the vocabulary issue. Opportunities seldom exist in a vacuum. Often, a small discovery leads to a larger opportunity. For example, an improvement in

Figure 5.1.   Implementing a Business Plan in the Private Sector

vocabulary that leads to better reading comprehension may also lead to better academic performance in other subjects where readings is critical to success.

Define excellence. Change requires a definition of excellence. Or, what is the organization trying to achieve? For a low-performing school, excellence may be increasing the graduation rate and preparing more students for college and the workforce. For a high-performing school, it may be providing students with additional opportunities in critical thinking and reflection in a global society.

Analyze and collect the data. Once excellence is defined, the next question is, "What are the data?" Data are important because it gives the organization a baseline as well as a point of reference from which to evaluate the current effectiveness of programs or services. Data are affected by both bias and beliefs. While one teacher may look at a test score of 70 percent as average, another may look at it as excellent—the difference is simply a matter of perspective.

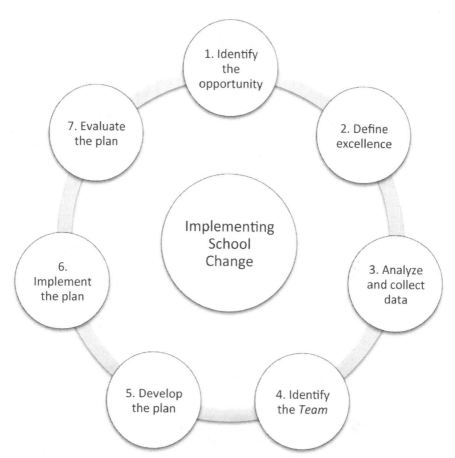

Figure 5.2. School Change Resource Implementation Model

For a high-performing student, 70 percent would be average, but for a low-performing student, 70 percent may be excellent work and evidence that those interventions and instructional technologies are working. This is also the time to benchmark the data (see chapter 4). Other schools or school systems may have similar data. Sometimes, it will become apparent that a change is not needed. At other times, benchmarking will highlight a change is needed.

Data collection is also important to assist in the development of a plan and evaluating its success. If data are unavailable, the change agent may need to collect data. Depending on the change, data collection may involve issuing a survey, conducting interview(s), and/or reviewing other sources (see chapter 3).

Identify the team. Who is ready to help effect the change? Or, in the most simplistic sense, "Whom are we inviting to help?" This may be an extended process. In some cases the culture of the school may be ready for the change. In other cases, there may need to be a "time-out" in the process to work on school culture so that the environment is conducive to the change. In either case, the goal of this component is to identify not only who is willing to help but what needs to be done to convince the other members of the school community to participate in the change (see chapter 2).

Develop the plan. The next component of this process is developing a plan to implement the change. In other words, "What resources does the organization have and what resources are needed?" For example, a school may have the funds to effect the change but what it needs is expertise. In working through this phase, what should become apparent to the organization are the "gaps" between what it has and what it needs. This is a key phase. Without resources, plans and goals die or, at best, are only partially fulfilled. No organization has unlimited resources.

Aligning, acquiring, and allocating resources in the most effective and efficient manner are inherently crucial to not only the implementation of a change but its success. If no new resources are available, this step may require the organization to look at other areas of the school or school system to see if resources can be reallocated.

This phase would include developing action plans, marketing the plan to staff and stakeholders, identifying how to measure the success of the change, and identifying how to both implement and monitor the implementation of the change. Once the plan has been developed the organization can move to the implementation phase (see chapter 3 discussion on CPI model and steps).

Implement the plan. The implementation phase requires a monitoring mechanism to allow for changes or modifications to the plan as well as the allocation and alignment of resources. For example, in implementing a new professional development model it may become apparent that not enough time has been allocated to provide peer mentoring to take place. A good implementation plan needs to have an element of flexibility.

Challenges to a successful implementation should, to the organization's best ability, be identified in advance. Allowances should be incorporated to allow for a "course correction" if a strategy is not working or needs to be refined. Marketing the change is also crucial. How will the team promote the change? What strategies will they use to change the school culture, if necessary, to allow for the change to take place?

Evaluate the plan. Change requires evaluation to monitor its success. As noted at the very beginning of this process, it is important to have a definition of excellence. Using that definition, we can evaluate the successes and failures of the change and plan. A key part of the evaluation needs to include an analysis of *effectiveness* and *efficiency*. Effectiveness can be defined as "how well we achieved the desired outcomes."

Efficiency can be defined as "how well we used the resources assigned to the task." In some cases, we can be effective but not efficient, in other cases the opposite may true. The goal of any change should be to be as highly effective and highly efficient as possible. This may not always be the case, however.

What is important is that we have that kind of entrepreneurial spirit that enables the change team to recognize and learn from failure and celebrate and invest resources in success. This is very difficult for most schools and school systems to accomplish. Schools do not operate in a vacuum. They are, by their very nature, public entities. It is difficult to admit spending $250,000 on a new reading program that doesn't work or shows minimal gains. This too is part of dealing with change.

"Ownership" is both a blessing and curse. Change agents want the school stakeholders to *buy in* to the process but it can also prevent us from seeing failure. For example, it is like the stockbroker who buys a stock at ten dollars with great fundamentals. For whatever reason, the stock falls out of favor with investors but still has great fundamentals, so the broker keeps it. Eventually, the broker has to take a big loss on the stock.

If only the broker had recognized that his own bias and beliefs were affecting his decision, he would have cut his loss. This is an important concept. If something isn't working and the change agent can't fix it, an alternative needs to be considered. Continuing to allocate resources to an unsuccessful approach only means those resources are unavailable for the next one. With all that is going on in schools, change agents need to recognize that it is *change* that is the constant and not *the status quo.*

MANAGING SCHOOL RESOURCES— A NATIONAL CHALLENGE

From a national perspective, there are a litany of initiatives that have been implemented to change school cultures and promote learning and achievement. In the 1960s, educators recognized that preparedness for school was important for success in school. The resulting change was the allocating of resources for Head Start and early childhood education. Unfortunately, fifty years later, resources still have not been fully allocated in early childhood education throughout the nation, even though research suggests there is a direct positive correlation with student achievement.

In 1966, the Coleman Report was issued, which recognized the influence of peer groups on students and their education (Coleman et al., 1966). This resulted in an emphasis on desegregating schools and the creation of alternatives such as magnet schools. The report indicated that student achievement was more closely related to family background than to school resources.

Gamoran and Long (2006) note that: "The Coleman report has played a strong role in shifting the focus of debates about inequalities from inadequate resources to the ways which resources are used" (p. 17). This highlights why the utilization of resources is key to implementing change.

No Child Left Behind (NCLB) focuses on the importance of teachers being well educated and knowing their subject. Hence, the current focus on highly qualified teachers, National Board Certification, evaluation, performance, and teacher preparation programs. Lastly is the growing body of research on a positive school environment that does not discriminate, provides a number of support services, addresses the needs of bilingual students, and is committed to graduating well-prepared students.

The question, of course, is, have these initiatives worked? The one thing they all have in common is that they have been "top down." All are attempts at change through legislation by the courts and/or legislation. Whether or not these initiatives to change how we educate children have been successful is a function of both the willingness and ability of schools to change.

One of the common elements of change in school systems is that it is often brokered. School districts are subject to a myriad of rules and regulations. Collective bargaining agreements often dictate that change must be negotiated. When the participants cannot agree on the type and rate of change, there can be dire consequences.

A recent example of brokered change through negotiation is the 2012 Chicago Teachers Union strike. The strike was the first one in twenty-five years and, other than compensation, the key issue was changing the method of teacher evaluation that ties teachers' ratings to the growth and achievement of their students and a longer school day. Mayor Rahm Emanuel noted, "The settlement was an honest compromise" and "a new day and new direction for the Chicago Public Schools" (Rossi, Esposito, & Fitzpatrick, 2012, p. 1).

Likewise, state and federal regulations often dictate change at the local level. No Child Left Behind (NCLB) and Race to the Top (RTTT) are both examples of the federal government's attempt to change the educational system from the top down. Has it been successful? At this juncture, the jury is still out. While almost everyone would agree that the goals of NCLB are noble, almost all educators believe that the timelines for producing measurable outcomes are unrealistic.

On a state-by-state basis, the criteria for student success and teacher performance differ. Some thirty-three states have approved waivers of NCLB. Some states have set performance goals at different levels for various subgroups of students. In Florida, Governor Scott came out against a plan by the Florida State Board of Education that would require 86 percent of white students but only 74 percent of black students to be performing at proficient levels by 2017–2018 ("Scott Sets Expectations," 2012).

What does the future hold for educational change in America's schools? Arnie Duncan, speaking about his second term as U.S. secretary of education said, "[I will use my] second term to continue to leverage education improvement at the state and local levels, with a new emphasis on principal preparation and evaluation" (McNeil, 2012, p. 1). Duncan went on to say that he thought that district-level innovation is important. So with the pressure on local school systems, all stakeholders must be willing to reevaluate, and reallocate resources to improve student achievement and graduation rates.

In other words, local school systems must be willing to change in a meaningful way. If, according to Duncan, two-thirds of the School Improvement Grant (SIG) schools have shown no improvement, then the obvious question becomes, "How do we allocate resources to promote change?"

THE RELATIONSHIP BETWEEN RESOURCES AND ACHIEVEMENT

Considering that the primary reason schools exist is the education of young people, the majority of the financial resources should go toward the instructional process, namely, the teachers and tools for teaching. Everything else is, in the strictest sense, in support of the instructional process. Just how much money is needed for schools to operate effectively is unknown. Hanushek and Lindseth (2009) found that the court remedies in Kentucky, New

Jersey, and Wyoming yielded virtually no change in patterns of achievement. As noted by Golab (2010):

- Elementary students in Bannockburn had the fourth-highest test scores in
  Illinois last year, but that achievement wasn't reflected in the pay of their
  teachers, whose average salaries ranked 242nd among elementary school
  districts statewide.
- The north suburban school district is one example of the wide disparity
  between teacher pay and student achievement that a *Chicago Sun-Times*
  analysis has found is common throughout Illinois.
- Just seven of the top twenty-five elementary districts for highest-paid
  teachers also made the top twenty-five in student achievement scores.

On the other hand, Ferguson (1991) demonstrated that financial resources
do make a difference in increasing performance. He found that the biggest
difference occurred when expenditures were targeted at instructional processes. His research suggests that allocating resources for such things as
higher-quality teachers generates the most significant increases in achievement. Darling-Hammond, in her book *The Flat World and Education* (2010),
noted that there are five obstacles that prevent the equal and adequate distribution of resources. They are:

- The high level of poverty and low level of social supports for low-income
  children's health and welfare, including their early learning opportunities.
- The unequal allocation of school resources, which is made politically
  easier by the resegregation of schools.
- Inadequate systems for providing high-quality teachers and teaching to all
  children in all communities.
- Rationing of high-quality curriculum through tracking and interschool
  disparities.
- Factory-model school designs that have created dysfunctional learning
  environments for students and unsupportive settings for strong teaching.

What can be said, at best, is the jury is out on the degree to which financial resources matter. Hanushek (1989) indicated that there was no strong
relationship between school expenditures and student performance. Hedges,
Laine, and Greenwald (1994) challenged that concept. They noted that finan-

cial resources do matter. In fact, to reach their conclusion, they relied on the same data most often used to demonstrate the opposite.

Among the most often cited research regarding "does money matter" is that of Hanushek (1981, 1986, 1989). He looked at data from thirty-eight different articles and books using regression coefficients to determine the effect of inputs on student performance. Picus (1995) summarized his conclusion as follows:

- There was no conclusive statistical evidence that pupil-teacher ratio or teacher education resulted in increased student achievement.
- There was a positive correlation between teacher experience and salaries and student achievement. Hanushek noted that neither of these relationships was particularly strong.
- Per pupil expenditures were not a significant variable in determining student performance.
- Administrative inputs did not have a systematic relationship to student achievement and there was little relationship between the quality of school facilities and student performance.

The National Working Group on Funding Student Learning (2008) postulates that there are some inherent problems with the way that finance systems currently target and link resources. They look at five different attributes of financing systems: resource target; the linkage between resources and educational programs; the resource management process; accountability; and the link between resources and student outcomes.

What they observe is that in conventional finance systems resources are directed toward district goals and there is no link between resources and education programs, spending is governed by categories, accountability is a matter of compliance, and the link between resources and outcomes is missing.

In what they have termed Learning-Oriented Finance Systems, resources are targeted toward students, integrated with educational programs, and effectively used for continuous improvement. Accountability is a function of student learning and the link between resources and student outcomes is transparent (National Working Group on Funding Student Learning, 2008).

In 2012, the Albert Shanker Institute issued a new report, *Revisiting the Age-Old Question: Does Money Matter in Education?* (Baker, 2012). Baker basically looked at three questions:

1. Are there differences in aggregate school funding reflected in differences in short- and long-term measured outcomes?
2. Are the differences in measured outcomes a result of differences in specific school programs and/or resources?
3. Does redistributing money or increasing the level of funding through state finance reforms lead to improvements in the distribution of student outcomes?

The answer to each question, according to Baker, is "yes." Baker noted that Hanushek's 1986 student has been the basis for the belief by many that money does not matter. He notes that African American and other subgroup scores on the National Assessment of Educational Progress rose over time as school spending increased.

A review of literature on productivity and the link between resources and achievement still creates more questions than answers. Even so, it is clear that the focus of the educational community is now centered on student outcomes. This will inevitably lead to more discussion on how to align financial resources with student outcomes in the most productive and efficient manner. In order for this to happen there will need to be a greater emphasis on data analysis and evaluation. Hanushek noted in 2003 that:

> If educational policies are to be improved, much more serious attention must be given to developing solid evidence about what things work and what things do not. Developing such evidence means that regular high quality information about student outcomes must be generated. In particular, it must be possible to infer the value-added of schools. Improvement also would be advanced significantly by the introduction and general use of random assignment experiments and other well-defined evaluation methods.

UTILIZING RESOURCES TO PROMOTE CHANGE

School administrators are constantly challenged to meet the academic and socializing goals for the students they educate. Whereas private businesses seek to minimize overhead and increase profits, public schools tend to maximize the utilization of budgets in support of increasing achievement.

In economically challenged times, businesses reduce expenses and increase efficiency to stay in business and attempt to stay profitable. For businesses, productivity is the key. School districts are not used to thinking of productivity in the same terms as private businesses. Schools tend to think of efficiency as simply making "cuts" to balance their budget. However, making certain "cuts" can be counterproductive.

Basically, there are only three methods of balancing a school budget: cut spending, increase revenues, or a combination of both (Wong & Casing, 2010). Unfortunately for most public school districts, the only viable alternate is to cut spending. Spending is the only thing a school district has total control over. So with these challenges, how do we, as change agents, align, acquire, and allocate resources for higher performance and productivity in public schools?

As Daggett (2009) notes, school districts need to focus "resources and accountability around specific tools, strategies, professional development, procedures, and policies that can be documented to improve student performance." He goes on to state that this is a subtle change from what currently exists—it shifts the focus from inputs (programs) to outputs (student performance). Education Resource Strategies has developed five strategies to help low-performing schools improve their chances for success (Baroody & Center for American Progress, 2011). Those strategies are:

1. Understand what each school needs
2. Quantify what each school gets and how it is used
3. Invest in the most important changes first
4. Customize the strategy to the school
5. Change the district, not just the school

Increasing performance and productivity are dependent on many variables. The key to implementing any plan is to first identify the parameters, needs, and options available. This process should be done in collaboration with staff, taxpayers, and other stakeholders. The second step is to identify the strategies that are available for achieving the outcomes.

Outcomes include not only those related to the academic achievement of students but the fiscal health of the organization and maintenance of a safe and secure learning environment. Following are some suggested steps in this process (Schilling, 2010):

• Establish broad goals
• Establish financial parameters

- Confirm educational needs
- Confirm facilities' needs
- Develop approaches and strategies
- Make choices

Establishing broad goals that promote sustainability and scalable success in student achievement over time is crucial to allocating resources. The natural inclination for most school boards and administrators is to address the most immediate needs of the organization. This, of course, ignores planning for the long-term success of the school district. The goal of every school board should be to provide equity over time and have a means of measuring it.

Like most bureaucracies, schools and school districts tend to maintain programs already in existence and have difficulty eliminating those that no longer are effective. Demographics change as well as best practices and student needs. Confirming educational needs is important in that it forces organizations to reevaluate programs in light of student outcomes. The result of such a process is that resources can be reallocated and realigned to promote student achievement in a productive and efficient manner.

Care should be exercised to comply with all legal requirements. Most categorical programs such as special education, response to intervention (RTI), and bilingual programs have specific requirements set by the state. RTI, which focuses on research-based interventions and instruction for general-education students, has been adopted by a growing number of states (Zirkel, 2011). RTI, which focuses primarily on improvements in reading, mathematics, and writing, may hold the promise of reducing costs by implementing early interventions.

There are several strategies to confirm an organization's current instructional needs. Among these is reviewing information that will shed light on which practices, programs, and policies have been effective and produced measurable improvements in student achievement and/or outcomes. Simply put, invest in what works. This is especially important in times of limited educational resources.

Shifting resources from less effective to more effective programs and strategies will most likely result in the least amount of harm to students. To achieve effectiveness, schools and school districts must have data systems from which to draw evidence and conclusions. One method of doing this is establishing a set of "dashboard reports" which shows achievement trends over time. Figure 5.3 shows an example of a performance dashboard.

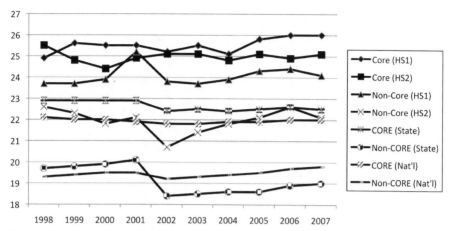

Figure 5.3. An Example of a Performance Dashboard

Change agents need to commit the organization to evaluating new initiatives from both an instructional and fiscal basis, determine if there is evidence that the results achieved are cost effective, and determine if the resources designated for the new initiative are better spent on investing in current programs and services. Often change agents just look at the cost of staff and textbooks. A better approach would be to include all costs: staff, benefits, professional development, supplies, textbooks, equipment, digital materials, facilities, etc. How many students will the initiative serve? Will there be a need for indirect resources such as counselors, media specialists, technologists, and so forth?

The bottom line in initiating a change is what purpose it serves and how it is viewed. For most school districts, financial resources are limited. For this reason, change is not about creating new programs, strategies, and organizations that require more financial resources but creating those opportunities through the repurposing of current resources or acquiring new resources for new initiatives through grants, competitive funding, etc. Toward that end, it becomes essential that the school community have good data from which to evaluate each component of its organization from the classroom to the district office.

Public school districts, like businesses and other enterprises, have experimented with various forms of budgeting to prioritize and allocate resources. Priority-based budgeting, programming budgeting systems, site-based budgeting, and outcome-based budgeting are attempts to link the budget to goals and objectives. These approaches are also being used to promote change in educational organizations by devolving the budgeting process to the school level.

Priority-based budgeting (PBB) is designed to bring about a cultural change in the way an organization does its budgeting process so that it's more effective and efficient, results oriented, and customer focused. PBB budgets are predicated on the idea that programs support instructional outcomes and/or school-improvement plans. PBB begins with prioritizing its programs and reviewing the costs of its services. A district no longer concentrates on how much money will be needed to maintain the status quo.

Another way of looking at PBB is to ask, "What are the core competencies you are supporting" and "In what priority should we support them" (Connolly, 1994). There are four basic questions that change agents need to ask when implementing PBB:

1. Why are we providing this service?
2. What are we buying for these services?
3. Who are we serving?
4. How much does it cost?

The purpose of prioritizing the budgeting process is to bring the district's spending into alignment with policy priorities. It also eliminates repetition of services, establishes economies of scale, and creates parameters for downsizing state government. The point of priority-based budgeting is not change for the sake of change. The goal of PBB is to assist the district in implementing what the stakeholders expect of their schools.

Site-based (school site) budgeting (SBB) gives authority to principals to allocate funds among various line items in a budget (Brimley, Garfield, & Verstegen, 2012). To be effective, SBB must involve all stakeholders in the process (see table 5.1). It does little good for the district administration to allocate funds on a SBB basis, only to have the principal of a school arbitrarily allocate funds without involving other administrators, teachers, and staff. The key to a successful SBB process is to let staff closest to the instructional setting set priorities and allocate funds.

As noted by Odden, Wohlstetter, and Odden (1995, p. 5), this requires that "teams of individuals who actually provide the services are given decision-making authority and held accountable for results." It also requires the cooperation of all stakeholders. It will not work in an environment fraught with "silos," where the math department is pitted against the English department

Table 5.1. School Site-Based Budgeting

Principals and their school communities receive funds in the following four categories.

Base School Allocation	Central Office Support	Categorical Funds Title I, federal, state programs, etc.	School Site Discretionary Funds
• Principal • Classroom Teacher	• Administrative/ Human resources support • Nurse pool • Security services • Custodial staff, supplies • Network, multimedia tech pool • Elementary prep time • High school athletics • JROTC program • Special education support • Visiting teacher allowance	*Allowed* • Instructional materials • Professional development • Substitute teachers • Hourly time • Supplemental teaching positions • Parent involvement *Not Allowed* • Clerical and support staff • Copier contracts • Noon duty • Athletic equipment • Medical supplies • Campus security • Building improvements • Custodial supplies	• All other campus staffing • Additional teachers for building level programs for at-risk students • Special programs— School/Library block grant, gifted • Materials and supplies • Hourly supervision, extended-day stipends • Smaller class sizes

for funds. With decentralization comes the responsibility to work collegially with all stakeholders.

Allocating resources under SBB must take place horizontally and vertically within the organization (Guthrie et al., 2007). As can be noted in table 5.1, not all funds can, or need be, allocated to the school. Some funding must be reserved for necessary support services as well as earmarked as restricted due to grants. To understand this concept, examine table 5.2 titled "School Discretionary Funding."

Based on the school type, there is a special allocation and ratio for discretionary funding depending on the type of school. Commonly, discretionary funding is used to promote signature programs, initiate new programs, provide unique co/extracurricular opportunities, and/or provide staff development.

The advantage of SBB is that it empowers administrators by allowing them to make decisions for the allocation of money to programs and positions that directly impact students. The key is to match needs with resources.

Table 5.2. School Discretionary Funding

Each school's discretionary funding is based on the funding ratio, amount per pupil, and the projected number of students for the school year.

School Type	Ratio	Total
Small elementary school, fewer than 250 students	1.5	$600
Midsize elementary school level 1, 251–399 students	1.2	$480
Midsize elementary school level 2, 400–750 students	1.0	$400
Large elementary school, more than 750 students	1.3	$520
Small middle school, fewer than 750 students	2.5	$1,000
Large middle school, more than 750 students	2.0	$800
Atypical/alternative	2.5	$1,000
K–8 and small high school	2.5	$1,000
Midsize high school up to 2,200 students	1.3	$520
Large high school, more than 2,200 students	1.7	$680

For example, the base level is $400 per student. A large high school with a projected enrollment of 3,000 students will have a discretionary allocation of $2,040,000 (1.7 × 3,000).

To do this, SBB cannot stop at the site level. SBB cannot simply be a means of distributing funds throughout a district without regard for how resources are distributed internally at each site.

To be truly effective, resources within a site must be distributed equitably. As one might suspect, SBB can be time intensive. Getting all stakeholders together to determine the distribution of funds within a district and within a site requires not only a significant time commitment but also knowledge of how resources impact student achievement.

Outcome-based budgeting represents the desire to tie performance to budget allocations (Kedro, 2004). Under NCLB and other federal initiatives, the focus is on student performance. To achieve performance increases, many states have moved toward outcome-based budgeting. Outcome-based budgeting requires that school districts have a clear vision, goals, and objectives. Budget allocations are then aligned with those goals, objectives, and outcomes.

Unlike other models, where allocations are generally rule driven, outcome-based allocations would be driven by the achievement of outcomes based on performance. In SBB, initial allocations are often determined simply by the number of students, special-need students, or other metrics not related to measurable performance data.

The *market dynamics* approach to educational resource allocation is relatively new and untested in the educational field. To allocate resources and costs, market dynamics determines what education is worth on the open market. Public schools operated by educational management organizations (EMOs) are growing in numbers.

As school boards contract out services to EMOs, there will inevitably be a comparison of cost and allocation systems. Assuming that EMOs offer an education that meets state and national standards, it is reasonable to assume that EMOs can be used to predict the true costs of an adequate and equitable education. In other words, if an EMO can educate a child for "x" dollars, then why can't a local school system?

EVALUATING THE USE OF RESOURCES

The fact is that most business ventures fail. Consequently, it is important to evaluate the use of resources with respect to implementing change in a classroom, department, school, district, or, for that matter, any educational environment. Change should always be viewed as a pilot. Some changes fail while others do not. How do we, as change agents, evaluate the success of a change? We start with the definition of excellence in the School Change Resource Implementation Model (see figure 5.2). The definition may include tangible or intangible benchmarks. It may be a change in test scores or behavior. As simple as it may sound, increasing attendance at school may be indicative of success.

A student's willingness to attend school may be reflective of a change in school culture whereby every child is valued. Likewise, growth in academic achievement may be seen as success. They key to both these examples is the magnitude of the change (effectiveness) and the resource commitment (efficiency) to effect the change. Figure 5.4 shows how to weigh the effectiveness of change. Note that ideally, any change would result in maximum results and the minimal use of resources.

With this background, what factors do we need to review to conclude whether or not change was effective and efficient? It is important to keep in mind that efficiency is not always achieved on the first attempt at change. A large initial investment, either in terms of financial resources or personnel time, may be required to implement the change.

Over time, fewer resources may be needed. Likewise, as staff become familiar and comfortable with the change, its effectiveness may improve. For these reasons, it is not only important to set a definition of excellence but estimate how long it will take to achieve.

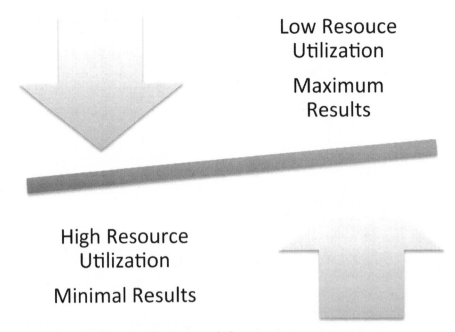

Figure 5.4. Weighing the Effectiveness of Change

Evaluating any change is always difficult. The first step in the process is to review the data. Data may be standardized test scores, interviews, behavioral assessments, surveys, or other appropriate instruments (see chapter 3). Was the definition of excellence achieved? Was it completed within the time frame anticipated? Were there any unintended consequences? Many times, making one change may have unforeseen impacts—good or bad.

A change in a professional development strategy to increase math comprehension may also lead to higher levels of parental satisfaction with the school. On the other hand, attempts to implement a new tardy policy may result in more absences if the consequence of multiple instances of tardiness is perceived by students to be more onerous than just missing a class. Unintended consequences need to be evaluated to make sure any negative effects do not outweigh any positive effects of the change.

An assessment of the resources used needs to be completed. Were the resources required within the acceptable parameters projected by the school or organization? Was the change efficient? Does the data show that a more efficient strategy may be available? During the process did the school discover any alternatives that should be explored? Last, but not least, is the change sustainable? Unless a change is designed to address a specific short-term

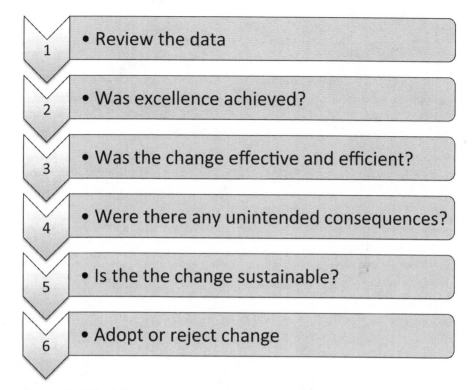

1 • Review the data

2 • Was excellence achieved?

3 • Was the change effective and efficient?

4 • Were there any unintended consequences?

5 • Is the the change sustainable?

6 • Adopt or reject change

Figure 5.5.   School Change Evaluation Process

goal, are there enough resources to sustain the change over time? Figure 5.5 summarizes this process.

SUMMARY

For resources to support school change, there must be participation and collaboration of all stakeholders. There is research that both supports and refutes whether or not educational resources make a significant impact on student achievement and the attainment of outcomes. What is critical is that educational resources are targeted in an efficient and productive manner to improve student achievement and attainment of outcomes. Change has literally become a national challenge.

School districts are continually being challenged to do more with less. The 2008 economic downturn has only exacerbated that fact. In order to obtain higher performance and productivity, school districts need to allocate resources where they make the most impact, being thoughtful to maintain intradistrict equity and adequacy.

The future of public school education in the United States is dependent on school districts and administrators finding more productive and effective means for obtaining educational outcomes (which have basically evolved to standardized tests). The economic challenges most Americans have faced these past few years only highlights the cost of education, staff salaries, benefits, and pensions. It is incumbent on the school community to demonstrate that "money matters." To do that, educators need to find what works and invest in it.

Implementing change involves a multistep process. The Model for Implementing School Change (see figure 5.2) includes identifying the opportunity, defining excellence, analyzing and collecting data, identifying the team, developing the plan, implementation, and evaluation. Acquiring, aligning, and allocating resources are crucial to the success of any change.

Managing resources to promote change means the evaluation systems must be in place to measure both the effectiveness and efficiency of the initiative. Schools must find a way to use failure to be successful. Under the current economic challenges, change may only happen through the repurposing of existing resources. Change is more likely to occur in budgeting systems where principals and school administrators have control over personnel, as well as financial resources, and have the authority to make decisions how they will be allocated.

CASE STUDY

"Aligning Student Outcomes with Educational Resources"

Saturn Unified School District (SUSD) is a diverse K–12 system located in a suburban setting next to a large urban city. You are the principal of one of the elementary schools in the district. By looking at the data for your school, one of the greatest needs is to improve the reading scores of third through sixth grade students.

SUSD is currently considering allocating resources to your school to purchase portable tablets through Title I funding, as 39.8 percent of the school's student population falls within the definition of low income. You are aware of several studies that have shown that portable tablet personal computers used in the classroom boost reading test scores. You are also aware of a recent study that shows that students who use portable tablet personal computers in the classroom score better in literacy tests than those who don't.

The data show that your school has not made annual yearly progress (AYP) for the last three years. One of the school's weaknesses is reading scores for children with disabilities. One of the school's strengths is in the area of mathematics, with children with disabilities scoring a 61.1 percent AYP score. The Hispanic population in your school has risen from 14.2 percent in 2001 to 30.2 percent in 2012. The low-income student population has increased from 11 percent in 2001 to 39.8 percent in 2012.

Upon completing some home visits, you noted that there were families that did not have reading material or even newspapers for the students to read. The school district has funded a number of initiatives. Those include the professional development programs, the lowering of class sizes, adding new positions (such as counselors, gifted and talented, special education teachers) as well as the grants (reading, math, social/emotional learning, and technology).

Your school has been identified because the special education subgroup did not make the target of 85 percent proficiency in math and reading. In addition, the group composed of all students in grades three through six failed to meet the 85 percent proficiency target in reading. Your school has been working to improve the school's academic program by offering professional development for teachers in the areas of reading and mathematics for all students and special education students.

EXERCISES AND DISCUSSION QUESTIONS

1. In the school system where you work or reside, how are resource allocation decisions determined? Is there a process for evaluating how well resources are utilized?
2. Referring to the case study, write one to two paragraphs on what data you would collect and what strategies you would employ to implement portable tablets into the classroom.
3. In your professional life, what choices have you made with regard to allocating resources to improve achievement? How did you determine whether they were successful?
4. Referring to the case study, indicate how you would implement the change using the Model for Implementing School Change (figure 5.2).

5. What should be the role of the principal, superintendent, and board of education in implementing change, allocating resources, and evaluating their effectiveness?
6. What is the difference between *effectiveness* and *efficiency*? Provide an example of a change that was effective but not efficient and a change that was not effective but efficient.
7. In reviewing the Model for Implementing School Change, what do you believe would be the most difficult step? Why?
8. What are the pros and cons of giving principals control over a school's operating budget? Is change easier to implement when principals have control of all the resources for their school?
9. Pick a change initiative with which you are familiar that failed. Why was it not successful? Is there anything that could have been done to make the change successful?

REFERENCES

Baker, B. (2012). *Revisiting the age-old question: Does money matter in education?* Washington, DC: Albert Shanker Institute.

Baroody, K., & Center for American Progress. (2011). Turning around the nation's lowest performing schools. Retrieved from www.americanprogress.org/issues/2011/02/five_steps.html.

Brimley, V., Garfield, R., & Verstegen, D. (2012). *Financing education in a climate of change* (11th ed.). Boston: Pearson Education.

Coleman, J. S., Campbell, E. Q., Hobson, C. J., McPartland, F., Mood, A. M., Weinfeld, F. D., et al. (1966). *Equality of educational opportunity.* Washington, DC: U.S. Government Printing Office.

Connolly, T. (1994). An integrated activity-based approach to budgeting. *Management Accounting: Magazine for Chartered Management Accountants, 72*(3), 32.

Cook, D. L. (1979). *Program evaluation and review technique: Applications in education.* Washington, DC: University Press of America.

Daggett, W. R., & International Center for Leadership in Education. (2009). *Effectiveness and efficiency framework: A guide to focusing resources on student performance.* Retrieved from www.leadered.com/pdf/EE%20%20White%20Paper%20website%203.25.09.pdf.

Darling-Hammond, L. (2010). *The flat world and education: How America's commitment to equity will determine our future.* New York: Teachers College Press.

Drucker, P. F. (1985). *Innovation and entrepreneurship: Practice and principles.* New York: Harper & Row.

Ferguson, R. F. (January 1, 1991). Paying for public education: New evidence on how and why money matters. *Harvard Journal on Legislation, 28*, 465–498.

Gamoran, A., & Long, D. A. (2006). *Equality of educational opportunity: A 40-year retrospective* (WCER Working Paper No. 2006-9). Madison: University of Wisconsin, Madison, Wisconsin Center for Education Research. Retrieved December 15, 2006, from www.wcer.wisc.edu/publications/workingPapers/papers.php.

Golab, A. (2010). High teacher pay no guarantee of results. *Chicago Sun-Times.* Retrieved June 23, 2012, from HighBeam Research: www.highbeam.com/doc/1N1-12F31B 7FE4BB7140.html.

Guthrie, J., Springer, M., Rolle, R., & Houck, E. (2007). *Modern education finance and policy.* Boston: Pearson/Allyn & Bacon.

Hanushek, E. A. (1981). Throwing money at schools. *Journal of Policy Analysis and Management, 1,* 19–41.

Hanushek, E. A. (1986). The economics of schooling: Production and efficiency in public schools. *Journal of Economic Literature, 24,* 1141–1177.

Hanushek, E. A. (1989). The impact of differential expenditures on school performance. *Educational Researcher, 18*(4), 45–65.

Hanushek, E. A. (February 1, 2003). The failure of input-based schooling policies. *Economic Journal, 113* (485, 64).

Hanushek, E. A., & Lindseth, A. A. (2009). *Schoolhouses, courthouses, and statehouses: Solving the funding-achievement puzzle in America's public schools.* Princeton, NJ: Princeton University Press.

Hedges, L. V., Laine, R. D., & Greenwald, R. (1994). Does money matter? A meta-analysis of studies of the effects of differential school inputs on student outcomes. *Educational Researcher 23*(3), 5–14.

Kedro, M. (2004). *Aligning resources for student outcomes: School-based steps to success.* Lanham, MD: Rowman & Littlefield.

McNeil, M. (November 16, 2012). Duncan sketches out second-term agenda. *Education Week,* 1. Retrieved from http://blogs.edweek.org/edweek/campaign-k-12/2012/11/Dun can_CCSSO_speech.html?intc=mvs.

National Working Group on Funding Student Learning (2008). *Funding student learning: How to align education resources with student learning goals.* Seattle, WA: School Finance Redesign Project.

Odden, A., Wohlstetter, P., & Odden, E. (1995). Key issues in site-based management. *School Business Affairs, 61*(5), 2–11.

Picus, L. O. (1995). Does money matter in education? A policymaker's guide. In *National Center for Education Statistics: Selected papers in school finance 1995.* Washington, DC: US Department of Education.

Rossi, R., Esposito, S., & Fitzpatrick, L. (September 18, 2012). Emanuel: Deal is "honest compromise." *Chicago Sun-Times.* Retrieved from www.suntimes.com/news/educa tion/15224814-418/chicago-public-schools-teachers-strike-over.html.

Schilling, C. A. (November 2006). *Entrepreneurship in education.* Paper presented at the Jamaican Association of School Bursars Annual Meeting, Jamaica.

Schilling, C. A. (March 2010). *Funding our vision: A five-year plan to provide excellence and opportunity for all.* Consultant presentation to West Northfield School District 31, Northbrook and Glenview, Illinois.

Scott sets expectations at the same level for all students. (October 20, 2012). *Daytona Beach News-Journal.* Retrieved from www.news-journalonline.com/article/20121020/OPIN ION/310199964.

Wong, O. K., & Casing, D. M. (2010). *Equalize student achievement: Prioritizing money and power.* Lanham, MD: Rowman & Littlefield Education.

Zirkel, P. (2011). State laws and guidelines for RTI: Additional implementation features. *NASP Communiqué.* Retrieved from www.nasponline.org/publications/cq/39/7/professional -practice-state-laws.aspx.

Chapter Six

Executing Change

OBJECTIVES

At the conclusion of this chapter you will be able to:

1. Understand how to identify needs and define excellence (ELCC 3.1, 3.2, 3.4, ISLLC 3).
2. Articulate the commonalities for change (ELCC 3.1, 3.2, 3.4, ISLLC 3).
3. Understand the concepts of urgency of change, a human-centered school environment, and incentivizing innovation (ELCC 3.1, 3.2, 3.4. 3.5, ISLLC 3).
4. Describe some practical strategies for executing change using the School Resource Model for Implementing Change (ELCC 3.1, 3.2, 3.4, 3.5, 6.2, ISLLC 3, 6).
5. Understand implementing and executing change from a district, school, and departmental perspective (ELCC 3.1, 3.2, 3.4, 3.5, 6.2, ISLLC 3, 6).
6. Describe the role of the change leader at each level of the organization in executing change (ELCC 3.2, 3.4, 6.2, ISLLC 3, 6).
7. Understand the impact of resources in executing change (ELCC 3.1, 3.2, 3.4, 3.5, 6.2, ISLLC 3, 6).

Schools and school districts are routinely challenged to establish goals and objectives addressing improvement, and in this process look for efficiencies in operations and reward systems for employees. All of these challenges require change. For more than a decade we have been deluged by the negative reports about our schools. This is due in part to the overreliance on standardized performance measures required under No Child Left Behind (NCLB).

Under NCLB, almost no school district is immune from failure. The fact is that all school districts show signs of both excellence and mediocrity. Contrary to popular belief, U.S. students generally outperform students from other large countries on international assessments of basic literacy. At the same time, however, millions of students attend school each day in inadequate facilities and many of the country's poorest urban and rural areas have schools that lack even the barest necessities.

With respect to change, the question is not how the nation's public schools are performing in relationship to the past, but "What will be our path in the future? Will it be one of excellence or one of mediocrity?" And if the country chooses excellence, what is it that we define as excellent and how do we change our schools and school systems to get there? How does the educational system develop change leaders (see chapter 2) and how do we actually implement and execute change in our schools for the future? Will the political bureaucracy that created NCLB lead educational change or will innovation and change come internally from educational stakeholders?

The Japanese, for example, have very different goals from those most talked about in the American educational arena. First, human relations skills are considered essential to the educated person. Second, academic knowledge is seen as just one part of the more comprehensive goal of developing *ningen* (human beings). This idea of *ningen* assumes a holistic approach to growth and learning. Can these same goals be applied to American schools to drive change and excellence?

There are over 13,500 school systems in the United States serving ninety-eight thousand public schools, employing 3.7 million teachers and serving 50 million public school students. Within this universe, there are incredible extremes: New York City, with more than a million schoolchildren, compared to the entire state of Nebraska, with 1.8 million residents but 540 school districts. With all this diversity, where are the commonalities we can use to drive and execute change?

COMMONALITIES FOR CHANGE

The *commonalities for change* refer to those concepts, trends, signals, and drivers that are shared by any school, school district, or educational organization. They are attributes that are global in nature but nonetheless must be

Figure 6.1. Commonalities for Change

considered when implementing and executing change. Figure 6.1 shows the commonalities for change.

The first commonality is the creation of a human-centered school environment. School environment reflects the culture, climate, and leadership of the school. Like the Japanese, human relation skills and teamwork are essential if we are to seek excellence. As the seasoned basketball coach might tell his players, "Ball hogs die." To paraphrase Lao-tzu, the founder of Taoism (Winston Churchill Leadership, 2013):

> The bad leader is he who the people despise.
> The good leader is he who the people praise.
> The great leader is he who the people say "We did it ourselves."

TEXTBOX 6.1.
SETTING THE CLIMATE THROUGH CHANGE LEADERSHIP

One Superintendent's Change Leadership

What is the fastest way to change a climate? Maybe it is changing a teacher's attitude about the students they teach. One superintendent took just such a perspective. Before any teacher in the district was hired he would meet with the teacher for ten to fifteen minutes. It was a pretty simple discussion. The superintendent would ask the candidate one or two questions to determine how the teacher would react if students in his or her class were not performing. Would the teacher attribute the problem to the students or would the teacher attribute the problem to his or her not finding the right solution to help the students learn? In other words, would the teacher *change* what he or she was doing or would the teacher expect the students to change?

The key to executing change is creating a climate in which staff believe "they did it themselves." To do this, there needs to be a human-centered school climate (see textbox 6.1 for an example of setting a human-centered school environment). Simply using task forces, committees, teams of professionals, and professional learning communities is not enough.

Just like individuals, committees don't always make the right decision. Sometimes they just make a decision. So the challenge for the change agent or change leader is to identify the context in which decisions will take place and to help individuals make meaning of the change (see chapter 1).

It is also important for the change leader to recognize the significance of the change and its effect on students and staff. Too often, administrators spend *leadership capital* for issues and decisions that literally make little or no difference. Leadership capital is the trust a leader has accumulated in an organization. When leaders go "against the grain" they spend that accumulated trust. Change leaders need to recognize (1) when to go to the mat for a particular change; (2) when to just give their best input; or (3) when to step back from the process and let it run its course.

Good change leadership promotes order as opposed to control. In other words, change leadership is about leading, not managing. It liberates staff to implement change. Kindergarten teachers learned this concept a long time ago—there are rules: share, don't fight, flush (Fulghum, 1989). Creating a climate that builds human networks and motivates staff is a key to excelling.

The second commonality is the desire to excel. The staff are not going to excel for something they can't appreciate, don't think is possible, or don't care about. Since excellence can be a moving target, staff need to commit to benchmarks that are both short and long term. These benchmarks need to be measurable in terms of effectiveness and efficiency. For schools and school districts, one of the biggest challenges in defining excellence is what can be referred to as "stretching the mind-set."

As a change leader, it is important to *stretch the mind-set* of staff from focusing on the status quo to the future. One way to do this is to have challenging definitions of excellence. Include staff in the definition of excellence. Challenge staff to excel. Whether educators like it or not, one result of No Child Left Behind (NCLB) was a set of challenging definitions of excellence. While many districts have failed to reach the goals of NCLB, most have made larger gains than they would have had it not been for NCLB's definition of excellence. How can this be applied to a school or school district (see table 6.1)?

This is an example of one district's goals that stretch the definition of excellence. The goals were bold, measurable, and were communicated to the public, which spurred dialogue and creativity in how change could take place.

The third commonality is the use of business intelligence, metrics, and dashboards to improve student performance and resource allocation. Data-driven decision making in schools is a relatively new occurrence in education

Table 6.1. Example of Goals That Define Excellence

Objectives	Evidence/Data Source
100 percent of students will graduate	• Master schedules that guaranteed access to courses and curriculum guide • Access to honors and AP/IB courses • Success rate in courses • Enrollment in courses
Full implementation of common core curriculum and assessments, pre-kindergarten to grade twelve	• Number of teachers participating in professional development for common core curriculum implementation • Classroom observation of teachers implementing the teaching of the Common Core State Standards
All students have access to challenging courses and to liberal arts courses (e.g., music, arts, languages, sciences, etc.)	• Establish multiple instructional pathways, general education and online • Variety of courses available • Vertical and horizontal articulation of courses • Percent of student groups in most challenging courses • Advanced courses offered with supports to ensure student success

compared to the private sector. Data processing software is now just catching up to the demand for information in schools. Unfortunately, most of the software that is currently available still doesn't meet most districts' needs.

Most schools require some type of *data warehousing software* in order to get the kind of business intelligence and information they require. *Data warehousing software* integrates data from various subsystems in a school district such as finance, student, learning, and human resources.

Once the data is within the data warehouse it can then be assembled and analyzed. An option to data warehousing software is real-time, data-driven software systems. These systems store data so that it may be assembled in real time and at specific times in the past, present, or future. This is particularly useful in studying patterns and analyzing resource allocations.

In the not-too-distant future, an individual student's achievement will be able to be correlated with human resource and financial data. Change leaders will be able to see if resources are being utilized efficiently and effectively. These types of reports (dashboards) are beginning to be incorporated into student, finance, and human resource software systems available to K–12 school systems.

Dashboard reports (see figure 5.3) are starting to be used by many school districts to disaggregate data as well as to report data to their communities and staff. For schools and school districts, dashboards are the business intelligence for education (see textbox 6.2). They provide real-time metrics, benchmarks, measure direct impact, and provide performance monitoring. They enhance the ability of schools and school districts to make data-driven change and decisions.

For example, they assist in identifying at-risk students, making evaluations, communicating results to parents, identifying in real time where

---

TEXTBOX 6.2.
BUSINESS INTELLIGENCE FOR SCHOOLS AND SCHOOL DISTRICTS

In the business community . . .	In the school community . . .
Provides business intelligence on customer spending patterns	Provides metrics on identifying at-risk students, interventions, and parent involvement
Identifies new products based on customer purchases; markets new programs	Allocates resources based on student performance, evaluation, etc.; markets results to stakeholders
Establishes targets for advertising, based on search techniques	Identifies opportunities for new programs and classes to meet student needs

interventions can take place, and assisting in the allocation of human and financial resources.

For purposes of dashboard reporting, a performance metric is a measure of the school's activities and performance. These would include demographic, finance, human resources, and instructional and operational activities of the organization. Just the mere fact of having metrics and reviewing them drives change. It empowers schools, their administrative staffs, and their board members to make changes that are impactful and not merely cosmetic. There are three basic guidelines in developing dashboard reporting:

1. Who is the audience for the data?
2. How will the data be presented (design)?
3. How accurate will the data be?

The importance of these questions cannot be overstated. To support change, accurate data needs to be available to the right people in the right format. It also needs to be transparent to all stakeholders. That is one of the primary benefits of routinely collecting, analyzing, and sharing data. Just think if the data was in real time and in a dashboard format. Turn on a computer and the dashboards appear telling you how your class, department, school, or school district is doing that day.

The fourth commonality is the development of a sense of urgency. A sense of urgency is, at times, very clear. For example, the state passes legislation requiring that 50 percent of a teacher's evaluation be based on student performance by June 30. In this example, the state has defined both the urgency and the parameters.

In other instances, however, the school or school system does not have a clear vision of what needs to be done or when it needs to be done. In those instances, the change leader needs to identify a process for determining not only what needs to be changed but also the urgency of the change (see figure 6.2).

In most organizations there are more needs than the available resources can support. Too often, schools and school districts try to tackle too many changes at the same time. This results in capital—both human and financial—being spread too thin. The result is unfulfilled needs, failure, and unrealized change. Furthermore, if repeated year after year, it leads to staff complacency. For this reason, it is essential that organizations concentrate on just a few significant changes that become the focus of the organization and align with the mission and vision of the school district.

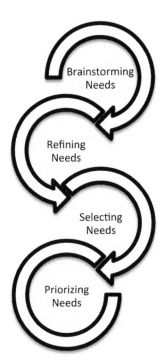

Figure 6.2.   The Process for Determining Urgency

The fifth commonality is the development of edu-entrepreneurs. Edu-entrepreneurs are both change agents and change leaders. Edu-entrepreneurs are individuals who are idea generators. They look for new links, have investors willing to buy into change, and most importantly take risks. They look to *exploit* change. What are examples of entrepreneurship? Examples would include charter schools, for-profit education, e-tutoring and online education.

Edu-entrepreneurs look to take an idea, benchmark it, raise capital, and then develop a business plan to implement it. In other words, they are looking to obtain maximum returns from their investment. Edu-entrepreneurs look for ways to raise capital from various sources. It could be new revenue sources such as grants, tuition, or private funding. It could be through efficiencies in noncore functions and/or outsourcing. Noncore functions are those that do not directly relate to instructing students, such as transportation, food service, cleaning, etc.

Every business, including education, gets a *makeover* sooner or later. There are many reasons why this may occur. For education, the focus on teacher performance, pensions, and salaries was amplified by the 2008 recession. For the phone industry, it was Apple's iPhone. Innovation promotes change. The question is whether public education can develop its own entrepreneurs, or will innovations come from outside the school community?

Unemployed teachers in Roseville, California, are starting their own self-funded private school in an empty hospital building. The teachers are paying the initial start-up costs with the expectation that other costs will be paid solely from tuition of about $6,200 per student. The school is hoping for 170 students and will focus on project-based learning (Kitaura, 2013).

The sixth commonality is the impact of technology. Technology can play a significant role in not only increasing productivity at every level of the education system but also in driving change. Educators can utilize open-sourced software, digital textbooks, and other technology-based resources that can provide low-cost and up-to-date materials.

Digital materials can be used to provide additional online learning programs for students, can be modified to meet a variety of student and teacher needs, and can create new opportunities for students in rural areas (see textbox 6.3). Of course, school districts need to ensure that all students have access to the technology. School districts also need to assess the total cost of ownership of technology, which includes not only the cost of the equipment but software, supplies, maintenance, and depreciation.

Technology can also be used to monitor and implement change. There are a number of open-source project management programs that school personnel

---

TEXTBOX 6.3.
THE IMPLICATIONS FOR TECHNOLOGY AND CHANGE

Learning will be powered by technology.

Technology will be used to assess student achievement and goals, and resource allocation.

Tracking the resources spent on each individual student, class, school, etc., will be used to evaluate the effectiveness of academic interventions.

Technology will be used to develop blueprints for educational reform.

Technology will be used to analyze the distribution and assignment of teachers to schools. Data-driven assessment will allow the best teachers to be equitably assigned to schools.

Technology will allow students to assess their skill sets against those needed for success at each college they are considering attending.

Technology will allow movement toward portfolio-based assessment systems.

Technology will eventually allow every state to collect data on every student so as to aggregate and/or disaggregate data.

More *disruptive technology* will be available to schools which will allow them to cut technology costs and allow for wider access for students, staff, and parents.

can use to track complex plans. These open-source programs include Gantt, PERT (Program Evaluation Review Technique) charts, and WBS (Work Breakdown Structure) charts.

There are also free open-source survey tools to collect data from staff, parents, and students. Free online tools such as Cacoo (2012) allow the creation of block diagrams, flowcharts, and mind maps. With this tool you can have a group of employees online simultaneously so the process of ideation, brainstorming, and discussion can be encouraged.

The seventh commonality is the motivation and encouragement of innovation. To be effective, school administrators must look at a multitude of models and strategies that create incentives to implement change in their schools and school systems. They must commit to providing the resources for faculty to acquire new skills. The status quo is changing rapidly. In fact, one thing is very clear.

Change is occurring as rapidly in schools as technology is changing our daily lives. And to make matters worse—depending on your view—school achievement data is becoming so transparent that every initiative, every teacher's performance, and every student's success or failure is under public scrutiny. If meaningful change is to be achieved, all stakeholders must be involved in the evolution of the organization in an active way.

And the key to future successes may lie in an entrepreneurial mind-set that rewards successes and innovation but does not penalize staff for risk taking and failure. We must provide school personnel with better information so they can act now regarding decisions that will affect students in the future. As a society, we will need to decide if charter schools, private educational corporations, for-profit education, e-tutoring, and online education will replace the underlying tenet of public education as we have known it. How can we encourage innovation and change in education and exploit it as an opportunity that addresses the needs of our students?

Developing a culture in which failures are accepted and innovation is encouraged will be difficult in the context of student learning where failures are frowned upon and excellence is expected. How can we use change models, strategies, and tools to be innovative and implement change?

Another innovative strategy that schools and school districts can utilize is shared services. Consolidating purchasing, insurance, or other services has resulted in cost savings and efficiencies in many states. Intergovernmental agreements for the delivery of low-incidence special education students and vocational education cooperatives are also common.

In some states, investment pools, cooperative bidding, state purchasing cooperatives, and shared fiscal services have also resulted in savings. Small school districts, in particular, which have limited purchasing power, small staffs, and fewer funds to invest are most likely to be the biggest beneficiaries of cooperative or shared services ventures. Following is a list of possible shared services in which school districts may engage:

Curriculum planning	Professional development
Custodial services	Purchasing and procurement
Employee benefits	Special education cooperatives
Energy procurement	Staff recruitment
Food services	Technical/Career education
Insurance	Technology services
Investment pools	Transportation services
Legal services	

The shared services approach changes the way schools and school districts deliver services and allocate resources. Fewer resources are allocated to non-core functions, allowing them to be used to address changes needed in core areas. This approach to change and resources is what might be referred to as a *repurposing* of resources.

The eighth commonality is the creation of a plan for a global future. Implementing the plan requires that safeguards be set to ensure timely responses to problems. Hopefully, any barriers are identified during the implementation plan and can be addressed through formative evaluation (see chapter 3). In developing the plan for parental involvement cited, there would be recognition that certain barriers may preclude its success.

For example, the parents' work schedules, language difficulties for non-English-speaking parents, and a lack of parent volunteers to interact with other parents may create difficulties. Obviously, careful consideration of any barriers should lead to alternatives to overcome them. In the example given, this may include translation or interpretation services, holding meetings at alternate times and days, and providing child care. To monitor the implementation, milestones may be set to monitor progress and success.

How an implementation plan is presented is also important. In some cases, a pilot study may need to be conducted to solidify the support of stakeholders for resources to implement the change on a broader basis (see chapter 1). In other cases, the urgency for the change may be understood and faculty and staff support is so great that large-scale change can take place immediately. In the first case, a pilot may be needed to convince staff a new reading program is effective for bilingual children. In the second case, technology in a school may be so old that the entire staff embrace upgrading it and are eager to implement the change as soon as possible.

In the private sector, staff development is a key component of change and a significant amount of resources are allocated for that purpose. Professional development in the private sector averages between 2 percent to 2.5 percent of payroll (Killian, 2009).

What makes effective professional development depends on a myriad of factors including the age and career status of employees, the culture and resources of the school, and who will be leading the professional development. Sufficient resources should be allocated to ensure that during the implementation process additional professional development could be made available to staff if necessary.

Obviously, changing the mechanisms by which services are delivered can be a daunting task. As noted in previous chapters, the essence of an organization is its culture. School systems seldom achieve anything significant without changing their values and overcoming the immutability of their culture (see chapter 1).

Unlike private industry, schools that perform poorly due to their culture don't go out of business like companies do but there are lessons to be learned. Take the case of IBM. In the 1990s, IBM's culture was expressed in its dress code: traditional dark business suits, white shirts, and ties. Their line of business was focused on computer, mainframe, and personal computing hardware. Lifetime employment was a guarantee, layoffs unheard of, and "Big Blue" was the leader in the industry.

But times changed and IBM was faced with either changing its culture or going out of business. In order to maintain its survivability, IBM refocused its business on networking, software development, and support services. They encouraged staff to adopt the "business casual" look of their competitors and, for the first time, IBM laid off large numbers of employees to restructure the company. The new IBM looked nothing like "Big Blue." In fact employees were uncomfortable, disillusioned, and questioned their future.

But the change at IBM was transformative and essential for the company to be competitive (Lagace, 2002). Like IBM, educators must be ready to respond to a changing global marketplace and be willing to transform their school's environment.

For schools, the data is clear. We have a more diverse population in schools, lower-socioeconomic-status students, more English as second language learners, and more students graduating who are unprepared for the current and future job market. Likewise, we need to recognize that teachers—like their IBM brethren—are probably just as confused and disillusioned and worried about their future. Performance pay, evaluations tied to student achievement, and layoffs due to financial shortfalls are all taking their toll.

EXECUTING SCHOOL DISTRICT CHANGE

So where does an organization start? How does an organization know what needs to be changed first? How does the organization set priorities and determine urgency? For many schools and school districts, the process of prioritizing opportunities is an arduous process. Some organizations use elaborate and protracted processes such as strategic planning.

The problem with a protracted approach is that by the time needs are identified and prioritized their urgency may have changed. Besides prioritizing opportunities, change leaders must also distinguish between the urgency of the needs identified and the willingness of the organization to execute the change especially when there is critical mass for the change to take place.

School organizations often fall into the trap of feeling that "everything is important." Give a group a survey using a Likert Scale (see chapter 3), where everything is probably important, and you will get just that—a list where everything is important and there is no distinction between the urgency of the items. Knowing that opportunities need to be seized in a timely manner means that school systems need a mechanism or strategy to prioritize the urgency of their needs.

There is a significant difference between systemic changes implemented by a school district and those by the school or department. School districts and larger educational entities tend to use systemic changes because they are cost effective and efficient. They are not, however, necessarily the most effective with respect to changing academic performance or changing school culture/climate.

For effective and lasting changes to occur at the building, department, or grade levels, the achievement and culture of each unit must be respected. Unfortunately, while change that is implemented on an individual building basis can be more impactful, it can also be more expensive in terms of staff time and financial resources.

Think of picking a new textbook. Simply picking a new book on a district-wide basis can be quick and cost effective. Doing so on a building-by-building basis would involve a much larger commitment of time, staff, and resources—especially if a different textbook was picked at different schools.

Aside from change that is implemented to be compliant with state or federal laws, there are two variables to note: the urgency and efficacy of the change. If we created a grid with urgency on one side and resource demand on the other, where would each change lie? Which changes are high priorities but present the greatest challenges with regard to procuring resources? Which changes require few resources to execute? Which changes in resource alignment and allocation need to take place to ensure success? Are there changes that are just "too big" (see figure 6.3)?

To better understand how to execute change at a district level, consider Pine Meadow School System. Pine Meadow has struggled over the past five to ten years. Like many school systems, Pine Meadow students have not made AYP

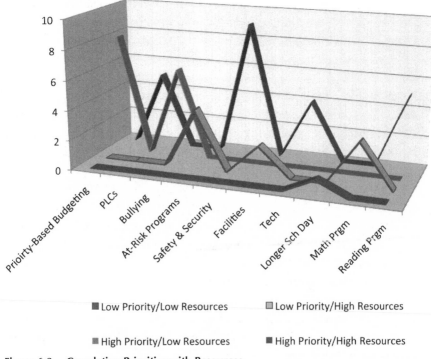

■ Low Priority/Low Resources   □ Low Priority/High Resources

■ High Priority/Low Resources   ■ High Priority/High Resources

Figure 6.3.   Correlating Priorities with Resources

(adequate yearly progress) as required by NCLB, and now the district must implement a system-wide restructuring of its schools, staff, and administration in an attempt to raise academic achievement and performance.

To identify the needs, the district has decided to do an abbreviated strategic planning model. As a first step, the district engaged various stakeholders to determine the priorities as well as their urgency and the level of resources needed for their successful completion.

As a precursor to the process, the district mailed a survey (see chapter 3) to parents and community members asking them to respond to a series of questions regarding the district's management, resource allocation, communication, and student achievement. The following stakeholder groups were identified at the same time: students, teachers, administrators, board members, parents, nonparent community members, and business community members. Each discussion group for the strategic planning sessions was composed of one member from each stakeholder group.

In conducting the abbreviated strategic planning sessions, the district chose to conduct most of the work over two weekends using facilitators to ensure maximum participation from all stakeholder groups. During the first weekend, stakeholders were asked to review the district's vision, review data on the district including academic programs, and review financial information regarding resources.

During the second weekend, stakeholders were asked to determine the district's priorities, the urgency of each priority, and the relationship between each priority and resources available. At the end of the weekend, each priority was *clustered* with other priorities based on both the urgency and ability to provide resources to accomplish the need. In order to identify the priorities and their urgency, the district successfully used a combination of *storyboarding* and *forced choice.*

Storyboarding (explained in chapter 3) was used by Pine Meadow to identify needs. Figure 6.4 shows this process.

The needs identified by Pine Meadow the first weekend were:

- Improve academic performance
- Increase involvement of community members
- Improve safety and security for students and staff
- Refine strategies for student discipline
- Implement priority/site-based management
- Address social/emotional development of students

Pine Meadows: Storyboarding Process to Determine Needs

1. Identification of needs by community members and stakeholder groups to restructure the school district and meet AYP standards. (Note: the question that prompts discussion and debate. In developing the question, it is often helpful to state it in the future tense to force participants to stretch their thought process. For example, instead of asking what should be the performance standards for students ask what should be the performance standards for students in 2020?)
2. Participants were selected representing teachers, students, parents, administrative staff, board members, and community members. (The greater the diversity the more effective the process will be. Different types of stakeholders bring different perspectives to the table.)
3. Selection of a facilitator for the process. The role of the facilitator is to move the process along, keep participants focused, and manage the time allotted.
4. Execution of the process. (To execute the process may take a half day or full day depending on the number of participants and the complexity of the task.)
   Following were the specific steps used in the process:
   a) The participants were divided into groups where each stakeholder group was represented.
   b) The participants were asked to brainstorm the issue. (Note: Give them plenty of time. At the end of this step ask them to write down their top 6 thoughts, perspectives, observations down on a poster-size sheet of paper. Have all the groups post their sheets on the wall.)
   c) One member of each group was asked to explain their group's list to the rest of the participants.
   d) One member from each group worked with the participants to eliminate duplicate entries on the sheets (make sure if the idea or thought is different, it stays on the list).

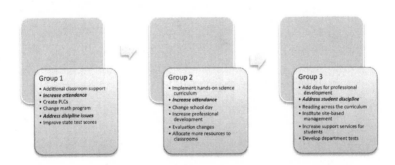

e) Each participant was given three sticky dots. They put one dot next to each of their top three ideas and/or issues.
f) Facilitators picked out the top ten issues based on the number of dots (note: sometimes there may be more or less).

Figure 6.4. Pine Meadow School District Goals and Resource Needs

- Review noncore functions for resources
- Close the achievement gap between at-risk and non-at-risk students
- Seek out business partnerships
- Retain, recruit, and develop high-quality staff

Upon determining the needs, the district then utilized the double-weight form shown in figure 6.5 to determine the urgency of each item. The total score for each issue is the total number of times (frequency) that item is circled. Results were compiled for all participants as well as for each stakeholder group. The district also found it valuable to disaggregate the data by students, employees, and community members. This is especially helpful

PRIORITIZING DISTRICT GOALS

SCORE Issue

1/2	1/3	1/4	1/5	1/6	1/7	1/8	1/9	1/10	1/11	1/12	1/13	1/14	1/15
	2/3	2/4	2/5	2/6	2/7	2/8	2/9	2/10	2/11	2/12	2/13	2/14	2/15
		3/4	3/5	3/6	3/7	3/8	3/9	3/10	3/11	3/12	3/13	3/14	3/15
			4/5	4/6	4/7	4/8	4/9	4/10	4/11	4/12	4/13	4/14	4/15
				5/6	5/7	5/8	5/9	5/10	5/11	5/12	5/13	5/14	5/15
					6/7	6/8	6/9	6/10	6/11	6/12	6/13	6/14	6/15
						7/8	7/9	7/10	7/11	7/12	7/13	7/14	7/15
							8/9	8/10	8/11	8/12	8/13	8/14	8/15
								9/10	9/11	9/12	9/13	9/14	9/15
									10/11	10/12	10/13	10/14	10/15
										11/12	11/13	11/14	11/15
											12/13	12/14	12/15
												13/14	13/15
													14/15

Figure 6.5. Double-Weight Survey Form for Determining Urgency

when looking for differences in priorities. Opportunities for change were readily discernible from the results.

Disaggregating the data also showed the district which groups were less reluctant to support a change (i.e., these groups would have lower scores for a particular need). Note that if Pine Meadow had desired a larger sampling, this process can be used to determine the participant pool and a larger group such as the entire teaching staff, administrative team, and so forth, could have completed the double-weight survey form.

The next step taken by Pine Meadow was to correlate and cluster needs and resources (see figure 6.6).

It is apparent in figure 6.6 that some of the objectives can be clustered by both priority and resources needed. This was an important step for the school district in that a number of low-cost, high-priority items could be identified. These goals could be planned immediately because they did not require additional or a significant reallocation of resources.

The final step from the district's perspective was to take each priority and define objectives and an action plan. Pine Meadow chose to use funneling (see chapter 1 and figure 6.7) in which needs are funneled down through each layer of the organization for definition and accomplishment.

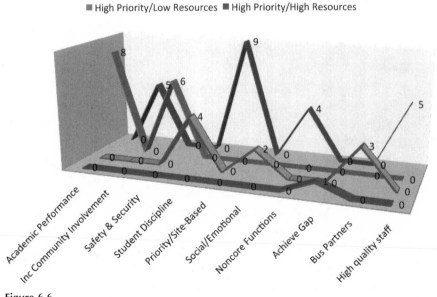

Figure 6.6.

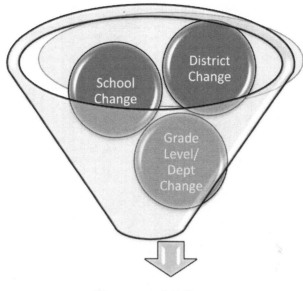

Funnel Theory

Figure 6.7. Funnel Theory

On a district level, each of the needs must be outlined on a global basis to provide parameters for the building and team change leaders. One of Pine Meadow's top priorities was to *improve student achievement*. Textbox 6.4 shows Pine Meadow's goal for improving student achievement along with the objectives and action plans. This information was passed to each school in the district for implementation.

Obviously, the other issue that Pine Meadow had to address was how to pay for change. How would resources be aligned and allocated to promote each of its goals? In Pine Meadow's case, that was a fairly simple exercise since one of the goals to emerge from the process was to move from a traditional top-down budgeting system to a priority/site-based system (see chapter 5).

Pine Meadow chose to provide each school in the district with discretionary funds to use to implement the change based on the type and size of the school (i.e., elementary, middle, or high school). In addition, the district supplemented district funds with federal and state grants (categorical funds) for use for professional development. To help support the changes, Pine Meadow's Educational Foundation made a commitment to fund individual teacher initiatives based on a competitive basis. Additionally, the plan committed to central office support for technology, data analysis, and other shared services.

TEXTBOX 6.4.
PINE MEADOW DISTRICT GOAL TO IMPROVE STUDENT ACHIEVEMENT

District-wide	Target Date for Completion FY2015

District Goal: "to improve student achievement"

Objective(s): What are my desired end results? (How will we look different in the future? What office-level changes, interventions would occur?)

1. Build assessments to assure alignment of curriculum to state and national standards.
2. Implement response to intervention (RTI) for K–12.
3. Implement and develop a professional development model for all certified staff.
4. Enhance and build positive relationships and collaboration among community, parents, board, staff, and students.

Action Plan: (Steps to be taken and included in your SIP, training for you, parent involvement, interventions to be attempted, community assistance, etc.)

1. Report out on assessments aligned to state and national standards.
2. Report out on RTI implementation and student intervention data for K–12.
3. Report out on the number of Professional Learning Community (PLC) groups in each building and list results from Smart Goals.
4. Report out on the quality of relationships within our greater community and the communication plan.

EXECUTING SCHOOL CHANGE

As noted earlier, Pine Meadow chose to use a funneling technique (see chapter 1) in which each need was funneled down through each layer of the organization. With this as a reference point, what is the school's responsibility in implementing change? As one of the schools in the Pine Meadow school system, Sunflower Elementary School was given the task of implementing the objectives and action plan shown in textbox 6.4 (Improving Student Achievement).

As a change leader, the principal of Sunflower Elementary School recognized that the first step was to research community-based reform. With the school having failed to meet AYP and the district working toward more community involvement, it was important to put in perspective what worked and what didn't with respect to teachers, community members, and improving learning. Textbox 6.5 is a partial list of the research the principal of Sunflower consulted.

TEXTBOX 6.5.
RESEARCH CONSULTED

Chenoweth, K. (2007). *It's being done.* Harvard Education Press.

DuFour, R., DuFour, R., & Eaker, R. (2005). *On common ground: The power of professional learning communities.* National Education Service.

Gabriel, J. G. (2005). *How to thrive as a teacher leader.* Association for Supervision and Curriculum Development.

Marx, G. (2000). *Ten trends: Educating children for a profoundly different future.* Educational Research Service.

National Association of Secondary School Principals. (2009). *Breaking ranks: A field guide for leading change.*

Reeves, D. B. (2004). *Accountability in action: A blueprint for learning organizations.* Advanced Learning Press.

Seashore, L., Leithwood, K., Wahlstrom, K., Kyla, L., & Anderson, S. (2010). *Learning from leadership: Investigating the links to improved student learning.* University of Minnesota.

The principal also decided to meet with teachers, parents, and other advisory groups. The school developed a single plan for student achievement that incorporated the goals set out by the district and then set about allocating resources accordingly. On a school-level basis, Sunflower decided to incorporate professional learning communities as an integral component of reaching the goal of "improving student achievement." The last piece of the puzzle was for the grade-level teacher leaders to develop the specific interventions and strategies for change.

EXECUTING DEPARTMENTAL/GRADE-LEVEL CHANGE

In review, the change process for the Pine Meadow School District and Sunflower Elementary School can be summarized as follows:

1. The district utilized multiple district-wide stakeholders to set the goals of the district, including their urgency. One of those goals was the "improvement of achievement performance." The district identified general objectives and action plans.

2. Sunflower Elementary School's principal took the goal, objectives, and action plans for improving academic performance created at the district level and incorporated them into the school's improvement plan:

- Completed research regarding strategies for implementing change based on input from the community.
- Incorporated stakeholders from the school to determine the best overall strategy for addressing the goal.
- Determined that professional learning communities would be the instrument to initiate discussion and change in the school building.
- Reviewed and determined the allocation of funding for initiatives to support the changes recommended by the grade-level team leaders using discretionary, categorical, and foundation funding.
- Determined the measures of success and excellence for evaluative purposes.

With this background, the actual responsibility for executing the change falls to the teacher leader in charge of each grade level within the school. At the teacher leader level, change is about having the right data, objectives, and plan to execute the change (see chapter 2).

In the case of Sunflower Elementary, the team leader (teacher leader) for the primary grades set up site visitations to other elementary schools that were failing AYP and had shown significant improvement in their academic success after restructuring. For example, team leaders looked at various strategies for improving reading that they felt would have the most impact on the overall improvement of academic performance. They identified multiple strategies.

First was a decision to implement "real" differentiated instruction in their classrooms for reading. To execute this change the teachers determined that they would need resources to purchase additional materials for each classroom. Their second strategy was to identify the need for additional personnel—specifically, one or two classroom aides who could assist classroom teachers. As a supplement, they also identified how the building's reading specialist and librarian could assist. Last, they identified strategies that could be shared with parents to improve reading as part of a community-based partnership.

Each of these strategies was quantified and submitted to the principal of Sunflower School for consideration as part of the site-based budget. At the same time, the team identified grade-level expectations and targets for success (evaluation guidelines).

Upon approval of the resource allocation, the plan at the primary grades was implemented and executed. At the end of each semester, grades and reading comprehension measures were monitored. The PLC format was used to discuss implementation issues and ongoing professional development. At the end of the school year, the cost of the program was compared with the original estimate as well as projected versus actual growth.

The data disclosed that the program had been successful but not to the extent the district desired. Correlating the data, the factors that seemed to have the biggest impact on reading improvement were class size and the amount of time spent by the aide helping classroom teachers. Taking that into consideration, the team and teacher leader proposed resource adjustments to the school principal who, in turn, submitted them the district office.

SUMMARY

Every level of the educational organization is affected by change. The roles that change leaders enact are dependent on where the roles fall in the organizational chart. Policy makers and school administrators must find a way to implement change in the smallest one-room school as well as in the metropolitan school system with over a million students. This presents a number of challenges to change agents and leaders alike.

The *commonalities for change* are an attempt to identify some of the challenges all school systems and educators are facing and will face in the future. These include:

1. Human-centered school environment
2. Desire to excel
3. Business intelligence
4. Sense of urgency
5. Edu-entrepreneurship
6. The impact of technology
7. Incentivizing innovation
8. Planning for a global future

Executing change is often a multistep process that includes the funneling of goals, objectives, and action plans throughout various levels of the organization. At the district level, it is important to identify the right stakeholders and overall goals of the district. At the building level, the focus should be on researching the strategies that can best be used to implement the change. At the department or grade level the focus should be on the strategies that will be most effective in executing the change.

CASE STUDY

"Executing Change"

As a final capstone project, identify a significant need for your grade level, department, school, or school district that addresses school improvement. Use the *Criteria for Executing Change and School Improvement* in Appendix B to formulate the process and plan for the change. Explain how this need relates to the school vision and mission and how you determined the sense of urgency to address this problem. Explain the facilitation processes and data collection you will need to initiate, implement, and sustain the change. Create an action plan that you can share with your administration, leadership team, and any stakeholders you deem essential to the change process.

Use each chapter to reaffirm your knowledge and skills as an evolving change leader to formulate this plan. Make the plan one that is of value to you, your district/school, and your community.

The following exercises and discussion questions will help you develop your plan in order to successfully execute change.

EXERCISES AND DISCUSSION QUESTIONS

1. In the school system in which you work or reside, what changes have been made recently? Discuss how they can be improved, lead to other needs, or are sustained.
2. Identify the factors that lead to successful change and what missing factors can lead to failure. What contributes to the success of the change? What contributes to the failure of the change? How does change impact the culture and climate of the school?
3. What differences or obstacles can occur in working with stakeholder groups that may affect change?—that is, teachers, support staff, administrators, parents, and community members.
4. How will you establish your change team to make meaning of the change and develop a shared leadership approach to change?
5. What data do you have available and what data is missing to analyze the need, and eventually evaluate the change? How will you create surveys and a needs assessment with your stakeholders?
6. How will you define excellence and measure the effects of change?

7. What should be the role of the principal, superintendent, and board of education in determining what changes need to take place within your school district, school, or classroom? Who are the formal and informal leaders that will impact executing change?

8. What functions in your school or school district would you consider effective and efficiently operated? Which are not? Are there functions that could be more effectively done through a shared service arrangement with other schools, government entities, or private companies?

9. If faced with the task of having to significantly reduce the expenditures in a school or school district, how would you go about it? Are there any services provided by your school or school district that could be provided in a cooperative arrangement with other districts, municipalities, or vendors?

10. How will your plan and execution of change support school improvement?

REFERENCES

Beyne, S., & Bedford, M. (May 2011). *Bending the trend: Lowering personnel expenditures for K–12 schools*. California Association of School Business Officials: California School Business News.

Cacoo. (2012). Retrieved from https://cacoo.com.

Fulghum, R. (1989). *All I really need to know I learned in kindergarten: Uncommon thoughts on common things*. New York: Villard Books.

Killian, S. (2009). How much should you spend on training? Retrieved December 25, 2012, from from http://effective.leadershipdevelopment.edu.au/what-percentage-of-salary -should-go-to-training/general/.

Kitaura, C. (2013). Teacher self-fund new private school in Roseville, aim for unique experience. Retrieved January 29, 2013, from http://roseville-ca.patch.com/articles/teachers-self -fund-new-private-school-in-roseville-aim-for-unique-experience.

Lagace, M. (2002). *Gerstner: Changing culture at IBM—Lou Gerstner discusses changing the culture at IBM*. Working Knowledge for Business Leaders. Harvard Business School. Retrieved December 25, 2012, from http://hbswk.hbs.edu/archive/3209.html.

Machiavelli, N. (1998). *The prince*. Chicago: University of Chicago Press. (Original work published 1532.)

Miles, M. B., & Louis, K. S. (1990). Mustering the will and skill for change. *Educational Leadership, 47*(8), 57–61.

Schilling, C. A. (November 2006). *Entrepreneurship in education*. Paper presented at the Jamaican Association of School Bursars Annual Meeting, Jamaica.

Winston Churchill Leadership. (2013). Leadership quotes. Retrieved from www.winston -churchill-leadership.com/leadership-quote-part11.html.

Epilogue

Leading school change requires many qualities and skills. Of most importance is credibility and effective communication so that the change leader is seen as trustworthy. This requires transparency in communicating the what, why, and how of change in a clear and ongoing manner. By demonstrating these skills, the change leader can inspire others to engage in change and be resilient during times of uncertainty and fear. This, in turn, creates a human-centered learning environment.

Feelings of individual and collective efficacy help people believe change is possible under circumstances that at first may seem impossible. Relating change to the mission and vision of the school helps create buy-in to change, as well as achieving realistic goals. In addition to personal qualities and skills, change leaders are accountable for results. Tangible outcomes in the form of data demonstrate school improvement that leads to incentives to continue the change process.

Leaders must be motivated to engage in the change process even in times of turmoil and organizational resistance to change. The change agent needs to reflect on ways to build intrinsic motivation so that feelings of enthusiasm and persistence are lasting. Interpersonal intelligence in working with others, in addition to intrapersonal intelligence in observing the inward impact of change leadership are both extremely helpful in overcoming personal and institutional obstacles.

Because job satisfaction must be taken into account when considering the motivational aspects of the work environment, the change leader should review the factors that bring about satisfaction and dissatisfaction to workers engaged in change. Also, change teams are needed to collectively address the roles, functions, and performance expectations when leading and implementing change in schools.

A cross section of formal and informal leaders who demonstrate various skills can provide a rich structure to plan, implement, and evaluate change. The change leader working with others will be more effective than the change leader who tries to address the challenges of change in isolation. The benefits of diverse points of view can lead to creative problem solving, decision making, and support for one another so that change management is shared, and change outcomes will positively improve the school.

The future of education will demand change because of significant federal and state legislation and the increasing needs of serving all students. Some of these legislative acts and programs include No Child Left Behind amendments (NCLB), Race to the Top, the Patient Protection and Affordable Care Act (PPACA), American Recovery and Reinvestment Act (ARRA), value-added methods, school-educator accountability, national common core standards, and educational privatization.

All of this legislation is an attempt at systemic change. Systemic change tends to be more cost effective and efficient but may not lead to the fundamental changes in student achievement that education is seeking. The biggest changes in student achievement do not come from systemic change but from local change (i.e., the change that comes at the department, grade, school, and district level).

This will require school leaders to keep abreast of new and upcoming legislation and the impact it will have on school and district improvement. More than ever, school leaders will need to be resilient in championing their associates and constituents for school change. School leaders will need to employ effective change strategies and business acumen skills to fully utilize available educational resources to maximize the cost-benefits of school programs.

For example, the cost of operating our schools today continues to rise and schools especially need to deal with the fiscal impact on educational programs and student learning. This is imposing a significant impact on all school districts across the country since many of them desire increased funding for operations and school programs for improved student achievement.

Moreover, many states have high deficits and pressing fiscal concerns and they will have to contend with managing competing demands for school resources. This will require states and school districts to change their fiscal and resource management policies.

In addition to states and school districts, these fiscal concerns will provide an impetus for teacher organizations to work with school districts and states to reform traditional programs. In other words, there will continue to be more and more incentives for innovation. All of this is requiring school leaders to become even more skillful in managing school resources, negotiations, collaboration, and change.

Another legislation impacting public education is the expansion of school choice. With the increase in lobbying for charter school funding, school leaders need to continually compete for limited resources. Also many charter school advocates are vigorously working to gain equivalent funding as public schools, which can increase fiscal pressures on states and local communities.

Moreover, programs such as Race to the Top are reinforcing competitive philosophies to school funding, educator accountability, value-added initiatives, and student achievement. All of this will require school leaders to be more vigilant in understanding and interpreting legislative laws and their impact on operating schools.

What does all of this mean? The only certainty about change is change itself. The school leaders of today and tomorrow need, more than ever, effective change leadership and management skills to deal with the myriad of uncertainties. However, the mission and focus of our work in the educational field is to meet the needs of the students, families, and communities we serve.

To stay stagnant and unresponsive to change will not prepare the next generation of leaders our society requires to accept not only the change issues we know exist now, but the ones that have yet to come in our global competitive society. Change leaders will have to develop new strategies to address the urgency of change in a flattening global society. With the right skills and strategies, leaders will continue to grow in managing and leading change, and realize the vital role they play in improving schools.

School Resource Websites

2020 Forecast: Creating the Future of Learning
   http://futureofed.org/wp-content/uploads/2011/07/2020-Forecast.pdf
Annenberg Institute
   http://annenberginstitute.org/
ASCD (Association for Supervision and Curriculum Development)
   www.ascd.org
Association of School Business Officials International (ASBOI)
   www.asbointl.org
Center for Safe Schools
   www.safeschools.info/emergency-management
The Change Leader
   www.cdl.org/resource-library/articles/change_ldr.php
Closing the Achievement Gaps
   www.edtrust.org/dc/press-room/press-release/states-can-close-the-achievement-gap-by
   -decades-end-new-education-trust-
Department of Labor Summary of Major Laws
   www.dol.gov/opa/aboutdol/law
Education Commission of the States
   www.ecs.org
Education Leadership Improves Student Learning
   www.wallacefoundation.org/knowledge-center/school-leadership/Pages/default.aspx
Equal Employment Opportunity Commission Laws and Statutes
   www.eeoc.gov/laws/statutes/index.cfm
Federation of Tax Administrators
   www.taxadmin.org/fta/rate/tax_stru.html
Great Schools by Design
   www.archfoundation.org/category/featured-programs/great-schools-by-design/
Leading Change
   www.educationalleaders.govt.nz/Leading-change
Leading Change from the Classroom, Teacher as Leaders
   www.sedl.org/change/issues/issues44.html

National Center for Educational Statistics (NCES)
    http://nces.ed.gov
National Clearinghouse for Educational Facilities
    www.ncef.org
National Conference of State Legislatures (NCSL)
    www.ncsl.org
No Child Left Behind
    www.ed.gov/nclb/
Teacher and Leader Effectiveness
    www.doe.k12.ga.us/School-Improvement/Teacher-and-Leader-Effectiveness/Pages/
    default.aspx
Teacher Leader Model Standards
    http://teacherleaderstandards.org/
Teacher Leader Voice and Capacity Building Lead to Student Growth
    www.edwardsedservices.com/teacher-leader-voice-and-capacity-building-lead-to-student
    -growth/
U.S. Department of Agriculture, Food and Nutrition Service, National School Lunch Program
    www.fns.usda.gov/cnd/Lunch/AboutLunch/ProgramHistory_4.htm
U. S. Department of Education
    www.ed.gov
U.S. Department of Labor, Occupational Safety and Health Administration (OSHA)
    www.osha.gov/
U. S. Environmental Protection Agency, Healthy School Environments (EPA)
    www.epa.gov/schools/

Appendix B

Criteria for Executing Change and School Improvement

Table B.1.

Criteria Needed to execute change	Chapter Where to review content and process	Local Resources Where to find resources to address the criteria at the district, school, or classroom level
Articulation of school mission and vision	1	
Identification of need; sense of urgency; facilitation of change process and tools	1,2,3, 6	
Data identification, collection, and analysis	3, 4, 6	
Identification of stakeholders, change leaders, and change team	2, 6	
Creation of action plan for school improvement; processes; resources; and evaluation	1, 2, 3, 5	
Reflection of change leadership and your role in the process	1	

After reviewing the criteria in each designated chapter, students are to determine where applicable resources can be found in their own setting and add them to the last column.

Appendix C

Template for an Action Plan

Instructions to create an action plan:

Column one provides the criteria to include in an action plan.

Column two describes the component.

Column three provides an explanation of each component.

Table C.1.

Project description	*WHY*	Include area(s) of focus and need / sense of urgency
Mission and vision	*HOW*	Discuss in relationship to the project
Identify stakeholders and change team members	*WHO*	Define
Create SMART goals (specific, measurable, attainable, realistic, timely)	*HOW WILL WE KNOW*	Process goals/results goals
Initiation steps	*WHAT and WHEN*	Planning meetings, agenda, time frames, messaging, communication plans
Implementation steps	*WHAT and WHEN*	Time frame, costs, resources, assignments, people responsible
Formative and summative evaluation steps		Data collection, analysis, creation of charts and graphs during implementation and at the end of the project. Dissemination of results.

Index

About the Authors

Dan Tomal is professor of educational leadership at Concordia University Chicago, River Forest, Illinois. He has worked as a public high school teacher, administrator, corporate vice president, and professor. He received his BS and MAE degrees in education from Ball State University and a PhD in educational administration and supervision from Bowling Green State University. He has consulted for numerous schools and has testified before the U.S. Congress. While a professor at Purdue University North Central he was voted the outstanding teacher. Dan has authored twelve books and over a hundred articles and research studies. He has made guest appearances on numerous radio and television shows such as: *CBS This Morning*, NBC *Cover to Cover, Les Brown, Joan Rivers, Tom Snyder*, CBN *700 Club*, ABC *News,* and *WYLL Chicago Talks.* He is author of the books *Action Research for Educators*, a CHOICE Outstanding Academic Title; *School Resource Management: Optimizing Fiscal, Facilities, and Human Resources* (with Craig Schilling); and *Human Resource Management and Collective Bargaining* (with Craig Schilling).

Craig Schilling is associate professor of educational leadership at Concordia University Chicago, River Forest, Illinois. He has worked as a public school administrator, systems analyst, and CEO. He received his BS degree in sociology from the University of Maryland, MS in human services from Boston University, and EdD in educational administration from Northern Illinois University. He has consulted for numerous school districts and has spoken and presented at over a hundred workshops and training seminars throughout the United States, Canada, and the Caribbean. He has served as an expert witness in school finance cases. Craig has served as the president of the Illinois Association of School Business Officials (IASBO), on the board of directors of the Association of School Business Officials International, and on the Illinois Financial Accounting Committee. In 1999 the Association of School Business Officials awarded him an Eagle Service Award for contributions to the profession of school business management. He is coauthor of the books *School Resource Management: Optimizing Fiscal, Facilities, and Human Resources* (with Dan Tomal) and *Human Resource Management and Collective Bargaining* (with Dan Tomal).

Margaret A. Trybus is professor of educational leadership and the associate dean of the College of Graduate and Innovative Programs at Concordia University Chicago, River Forest, Illinois. She has worked as a public high school teacher, department chair, curriculum director, director of school improvement, director of grants and special projects, and assistant superintendent in four diverse school districts. She received her BFA degree from Mundelein College, MEd from University of Illinois, and EdD Curriculum and Instruction from Loyola University Chicago. She is the president of Illinois Association of Supervision and Curriculum Development, vice president of Illinois Council of Professors of Educational Administration, and serves on the International Editorial Board of Delta Kappa Gamma Society International. Having authored numerous articles on school improvement and change, she has presented, consulted, and provided training workshops on this topic for school districts, regional offices of education, administrator academies, and professional organizations nationally and internationally.